Knock the Socks off Your Audience

Delivering Presentations with Power and Passion, to Audiences Large and Small

By Tiffanie Kellog

Table of Contents

Knock the Socks off Your Audience

Here I sit in the audience, squirming in my chair, listening to yet another person drone on and on. What am I doing? Checking my phone for the tenth time in the past 2 minutes. The time is just crawling. Why, oh, why do I have to endure this? Aren't there millions of other things I need to do? Wow, the second minute of a ten-minute presentation and I'm already falling asleep. Does he really think we need all these numbers? Why must he... zzzzzzzzzzz...

You thought the boring lectures were over when you finished school. Unfortunately, we have all sat in the audience while a presenter almost puts us to sleep, where it seemed he or she wanted to usher in the golden age of boredom. It sucked.

Personally, I am tired of those boring presentations. There is no reason for them to exist. *Knock the Socks off Your Audience* is here to ensure that the people listening to you will be waiting anxiously on the edge of their seats to hear what you have to share, not drooling on their neighbor's shoulder.

This is not just another book on presentations. ...well, okay, it kind of is. So why should you read this one? Because, I said so! Ok, just kidding – kinda.
When this book was only in my mind, I asked myself the

same question. Why another book on presentations? I know that there are AMAZING books out there - on technique, being a better speaker, engaging the audience, growing your speaking business and so on. What they are missing, though, is THE MOST IMPORTANT THING to do when speaking!

In watching thousands of presentations over the past decade, I've identified one thing that truly sets some people apart. At the beginning of the book, we will explore this key to making your public speaking stand above that of the crowd.

Before I get to what that is, it is important for us to examine WHY people present. Some people speak to help grow their business, while others use presentations to share a passion or message. When I poll an audience, I get dozens of answers. They all boil down to one simple reason: **when you speak, the goal is to magnetize people. You want the audience to be positively drawn to you and your ideas.**

Why? If your message is sound, why does it matter if your audience is drawn to you personally? The truth is the majority of people want to surround themselves and work with people that they LIKE! Your presentation can be a step towards becoming someone they *Know*, *Like*, and *Trust*.

First and foremost, magnetizing the audience must be at the top of your mind as you move forward with developing, crafting, and, most especially, delivering your presentation.

The first step is to be yourself. As you speak, be who you

are… Perfection is unnecessary. Keep this at the top of your mind as you move forward… Without it, you won't be able to magnetize your audience.

We are now ready to dive in and explore the #1 thing that isn't mentioned in most other books but should be in EACH and EVERY presentation you deliver.

Are YOU ready to *Knock the Socks off Your Audience*?

#eTiffanie: When you speak, your goal is to magnetize the audience, positively drawing them to you.

What's an #eTiffanie?

A note when reading this book, throughout you will encounter **#eTiffanie**s.

Of course, you're probably wondering, "What on earth is an **#eTiffanie**?" Well, originally the plan was to use the phrase **Tiffanie's Tips**, crucial points to pull from each section.

Instead, William Mellas, a financial advisor and client of mine, coined the phrase **#eTiffanie** a few years ago. He came up with it as a play on the word "epiphany", a sudden, intuitive perception of, or insight into, the essential meaning of an event or circumstance, usually initiated by some simple, commonplace experience.

Instead of epiphany, insert TIFFANIE, and what you are left with is an **#eTiffanie** — an epiphany from Tiffanie!

I will typically take notes on the inside covers of books, including my favorite bits and my own thoughts. Of course, I end up with highlights, notes scribbled in the margin, dog-eared pages, and tabs throughout the book too. That's why I've left a couple of blank pages in the back for all of the #eTiffanie's – and your own epiphanies - that you will gain while reading this book!

The #1 Thing to Do in EVERY Presentation: Telling Your Story

What drives you?
Why do you do what you do?
What is your story?

Your STORY, the reason you do what you do, needs to be at the beginning of every presentation you give. It doesn't matter who you are speaking to, whether it's a single person such as a prospect or referral source, an intimate group around a table, or a large audience. Each presentation should start with your STORY.

Although it may not be the first thing out of your mouth, you will want to share your inspiration for your business early in your talk. Why is this?

#eTiffanie: The thing that drives you to do what you do, your STORY, is crucial in getting people to connect with you.

Knowing your background has a tremendous impact in setting your presentation apart from everyone else that does what you do! By starting with your STORY, you will open yourself up to the audience, and, hopefully, help them to relate to you.

Now, while many people will connect, there may be a few who won't. And you know what? That is okay! You want to work with people who share your values and understand your motivations, while avoiding those who don't. The latter often become the clients who drive you nuts.

Sharing your story is not a new concept. People have talked about sharing your STORY for ages, sometimes calling it your WHY. Why, then, are we devoting the longest chapter of the book to the topic?
It is crucial in connecting with the people in your network (prospects, clients, and referral sources). This should be a fundamental technique in your marketing campaign, even though so many people overlook it. Because of the importance of the STORY, this chapter is dedicated to it. It will help you connect, and succeed, in your presentations. When the idea was first introduced to me, I had no clue what my story was, nor did I want to share the emotional aspects of myself in the business realm. I was resistant for quite a while.

I tried to come up with my STORY on my own. I kept running into a mental block. I could not come up with what my WHY was. I was unable to find that emotional connection between my past and why I did what I did. I knew the path that took me there, though I felt no connection. It was only after working one on one with Tom Fleming, a facilitator from Asentiv® and my current mentor, that I was able to be able to clearly articulate my STORY. Since I have found it, I am always sharing my STORY. When I share, people can see what motivates me, what I am looking to help create with others.

Every couple of years, I do seem to have another piece of the story, which had been forgotten, come back to me. As I recall those memories, I weave them into the STORY, making it more powerful and impactful.

Today, I enjoy working with entrepreneurs to help them discover their story. While I wish I could give you an exercise that you could do on your own to uncover your story, I find I typically need to talk someone through the process, whether it be via phone, Skype, or in person. Whether it is a coach or a close friend, find someone who can help you really dig down and find what makes you do what you do.

I do find, though, that hearing others' stories can help us at least identify what the story could be like, if one does not have theirs yet, or help us refine and communicate our story if we do. Over the next several pages, I want to share with you a couple of examples from real entrepreneurs. As you will read in the tips, you may want to have a short, medium and full length version.

My Story:

I grew up in the country, on 4 acres, with very few neighbors, which meant that I spent most of my time with my family, my mother and father, brother & sister. We enjoyed spending time playing in the grass, swimming in the pool, simply enjoying each others' company. We were and are very close.

In 1995, we moved to Charlotte, North Carolina, where I finished high school and got a degree from Queens University in business. Out into the real world I went and got that first "career" job, with a salary, benefits and vacation pay.

In March of 2003, two things happened that dramatically impacted my life. First, the company I was working for restructured the company, and my position was eliminated. The bright side was that I was offered a very nice severance package. Second, in the same month, my mother, who had been battling breast cancer for the previous 17 months, was given a terminal diagnosis. They were stopping chemotherapy, no other treatments to try, and we were told to enjoy the short time (if we were lucky, weeks) that we had left.

I never thought I would be the type that enjoyed, and was even happy, being unemployed, but it was one of the best things that could have happened. I was able to spend each and every day with my mother. Then on Mother's Day weekend, she was in the hospital, and we did not think she would wake up again. She did, and after a little bit longer in hospice care, we were able to bring her back home.

Our days were simple. On days she did not feel well, I would crawl into bed with her as we watched judge shows for hours. On days she felt a little bit better, we could get her out of the room and watch TV with the family, enjoy a meal, or even do a crossword puzzle, which my mother, sister and I loved to do together for years, though my sister or I would have to write the answers as her hand shook too much.

I remember one day she felt great! It was days before her birthday, and it was gorgeous outside. We got her into her wheelchair, made sure we had the oxygen tanks for her, and went outside to take a walk. In her neighborhood in Charlotte, there were numerous hills. Occasionally, I would hop on the back of the wheelchair so we could glide toward the bottom of the hill, sometimes putting our hands up as if we were on a rollercoaster ride. At the end of the walk, I was sweaty and exhausted, and my mom looked so happy.

A couple days later on July 10th, we celebrated her 47th birthday. Friends and family were there to celebrate the amazing woman, my mother. We were able to spend 3 ½ months together. On July 13th, she fell asleep and never woke again.

After my mother's celebration of life party, I was left wondering, what am I going to do with my life? I had lost my best friend, my mother, and I did not have a job.

During my mother's illness, a friend of the family, Jackie, would come over and visit. While most people were limited to nights and weekends because they worked, her schedule was more flexible because she was an entrepreneur. I thought that was what I wanted. I did not want to be tied down with a 9-5 job. I was lucky to be unemployed while my mom was dying, and I didn't want that to go away.

I decided I was going to start my own business!

I picked up my life, bought an embroidery machine, and moved to Florida on Halloween of 2003. I started my business Thread Art.

I had visions of sleeping in late, taking off early, 3 and 4 day weekends – the dream of what I thought life could be as an entrepreneur! Instead, what I found is just because I had a business didn't mean I had any business. Quickly, I became a slave to my business, working and working and working. I did the only thing that I knew to do to put food on the table and keep the roof over my head, I started cold calling. And I kept cold calling...

Until a phone call came in March of 2005. There was a gentleman on the phone named Darren who asked me if I would like to come to a networking event with him. After blowing him off a few times, I finally submitted and went. It was like the clouds parting on a gloomy day, with the sun shining down. There was a room full of people there with the potential to pass me referrals. I was in! Over the upcoming months I joined a BNI chapter and my local Chamber of Commerce. I attended some women's networking lunches and went to expos. I started networking, networking, networking. Within a year, I was able to quit cold calling (which had been 80% of my week prior to networking). I kept getting busier, busier, busier, which was great, except now I was working ALL THE TIME.

I did not become an entrepreneur to work all the time. I became an entrepreneur so I could enjoy life to its fullest each and every day.

In the fall of 2006, I finally reluctantly agreed to take a program I had been hearing about for over a year, the Certified Networker Program. I had hesitated in the past, as it was a heavy time commitment as well as more money than I had spent on any educational program, other than college.

Within the first 4 modules (out of 12 modules), I was able to make the tuition for the course back through a single technique I learned from Tom. I kept implementing what I learned, and over the following year, I was able to cut my work week from 7 days a week to 4 days a week, get my husband to quit his job and come work with me, and we were making more money than before the Certified Networker. I was finally beginning to be able to live the life I had envisioned.

For me, 4 days of work a week leaves a lot of free time, and I had the opportunity to start sharing the Ignite Your Business program (formally the Certified Networker Program). At first, I was helping out, training a module or so each month. The amount of time I spent training increased and by 2009, I decided what I wanted to do with my life was to help work with entrepreneurs to increase their referrals, leading to creating the life they desire, sooner. They gain the time to spend with the people they love, doing the things that they love to do!

We don't know if we have 3 ½ weeks, 3 ½ months, 3 ½ years even to do what we want. Why put off for decades what we can do sooner?

I work with entrepreneurs to help them have amazing businesses and spectacular lives.

As you are reading, did you connect with any part of the story? What piece(s) resonated with you? What stood out?

Keep that in mind as we read through these next examples.

Sara Chiarilli, owner of Artful Conceptions
<u>www.artfulconceptions.net</u>

Growing up, home meant perfection. My parents worked and traveled all the time, meaning that we spent a good amount of time with relatives and neighbors. It was rare to spend my birthday with my parents as they were usually away. I can remember one time spending the week of my birthday with the neighbor for whom I would babysit. There were many times that I would receive a note at school letting me know who would be picking me up that day. We always had to know our safe word so that if we were being picked up by someone we didn't know we had a way to know we were "safe". The constant uncertainty made me feel anxious and nervous. I was always searching for a place that was home to me. I was looking for a place that was safe and consistent. I was looking for a place that didn't just look perfect on the outside but was warm and fuzzy and gave you a hug when I came through the door. As an Interior Designer, it is now my goal to create that safe, warm and inviting home for my clients so that they can thrive.

Rob Kellog, owner of Fast Break Marketing (www.fastbreakmarketing.com)

I was always one of the tallest kids growing up. It seemed natural that I would play basketball. It wasn't enough just to play, though, I wanted to win!

I practiced hard, making sure I had the skills needed when I stepped on the court. After a couple years, I got pretty good, and I even was making a name for myself. People knew who I was before I stepped on the court. My scouting report read:

#50 – Rob Kellog: tall thin kid, posts up well, WILL DUNK ON YOU.

And I would.

Before each game, I would psych myself up, listening to the music. Before the game even started, my opponents could see the focus in my eyes, and I could see the fear in theirs.

My confidence helped increase their fear and helped me to be a better competitor and WIN!

What I realize today is that I help my clients win through their marketing. Together, we work together to create the right *game* plan that will help them be successful in growing their business by keeping their current clients and gaining new ones. Before the prospects even sit down to talk to my client, the prospect will know about you, the brand and reputation preceding them.

How do my clients win?

I help them have more: more money, more revenue, more referrals.

Shawn Yesner, owner of Yesner Law (www.yesnerlaw.com)

Growing up, I dealt with books and homework, tests, and band practice, but, mostly, I dealt with a bully. He was not just any bully – he was my bully and he tormented me non-stop for 9 years over a 12-year period of my life. Some of the more tame things that he would do: wrap me in packing tape (at that time, I had a full head of hair), hit me, sit on me, and kick me, and that was just the physical stuff. He also insulted me and put me down publicly every chance he could.

In fact, one day I remember walking from home to school. (I only lived two blocks from high school.) My bully thought it would be funny to drive his car up onto the sidewalk and chase me for a few houses. What seemed to him to be a prank, felt to me like he was trying to run me over. As soon as I saw the car skid from the street onto the sidewalk, I started to run. Although I only ran for a few moments, it felt like I ran for miles. I remember being so afraid! When I turned to look back to see where he was, I fell! I started crawling as fast as I could towards the nearest tree thinking, "He won't run me over if it means damaging his car, and, if he does run me down, at least he'll hit the tree too and there will be proof for my parents so they'll know how I died. At the very last minute, as I tried to catch my breath, he swerved and went back onto the main road, barely missing me and the tree, and leaving skid marks in the grass. I could hear him laughing in the distance as he continued to drive to school. It took me about 15 minutes to catch my breath, make sure he was out of view, and get to school. I was so scared, I didn't even realize my clothes were dirty and I was bleeding from the cuts and scrapes of falling and then grabbing onto that tree.

The only other time I received any relief was our family vacations to Walt Disney World in Orlando, Florida. I was so excited. I *loved* the feeling of being away on vacation, where anything could happen, free from the stress of everyday life, school, projects, books and homework, and especially being away from my bully. I felt the pressures of my life literally lift off my shoulders! I loved that bullies (and mine in particular) were nowhere to be found, not even mosquitoes were allowed on grounds at Disney. Today, I get that same excitement going on vacation with my kids and seeing Disney World through my sons' eyes.

I finally overcame my bully. He was a drummer like me and I eventually learned that his bullying was simply jealousy. We eventually, during college, became friends!

What I realize today is as a Bankruptcy Attorney I help my clients get control of the financial bullies in their lives so they can feel those stresses and burdens literally float off of their shoulders. This helps them live the lifestyle of their dreams. I love when my clients feel that same excitement of waking up in the morning, as if every day was the first day of vacation for them, too.

Hopefully, these examples have sparked some thoughts regarding your own business and your own story.

As you may have noticed, each story focuses on what drives and inspires you.
What inspires you each and every morning when you get out of bed? What drives you?

There are several additional example stories, of all lengths, at the back of the book in the bonus section.

Tips for Sharing Your Story

As you begin to craft your STORY, keep in mind:

- There is power in sharing the WHY you do something instead of just WHAT you do. When you open yourself up and share what drives you, you are showing that a level of passion sets you apart from your competition.
  Use your story as the foundation for your marketing. Be consistent in sharing your why throughout.

- The STORY is *not* about HOW you got into the profession you are currently in. While interesting, that's not where we're going with this. Your STORY is about what DRIVES you to do what you do. This often has nothing to do with the profession that you are in. Rather, it focuses on how you gain satisfaction by ***creating benefits for people***!

#eTiffanie: Your STORY helps people see your passion for what you create for your clients.

- Your STORY typically comes from something that happened early on in your life, perhaps when you were a child. At first, you may only remember a connection from a decade or so ago – but keep thinking! There are often patterns in our lives, themes that repeat over and over again as we age. As these tend to be recurring, they reinforce what and why we believe. Find their source.

- Your STORY needs to be emotional. There are many emotions to choose from, ranging on the spectrum from happy to tragic. Your goal is to share the emotions that help build the strongest connection with your listeners. Could the emotion that you share in your story include joy or anger, fear or sadness? Perhaps there was surprise or kindness, remorse, happiness and love, terror, ecstasy. There are so many that people will connect with.

- As you are sharing your STORY, you will want to RELIVE the story.
  What does that look like?
  Take the listeners back in time to when the specific memory occurred. Give them specific

details, like your age, and use the language that you would have used at that age. What are the things you noticed? Where were you? Paint us a picture using sensory details, like smell and taste. You do not want to just look over your shoulder and repeat events. Make us feel as if we were there experiencing a part of your past with you.

- Occasionally, people will feel as if they are casting blame or playing the victim when they describe the actors who had an impact on their story. Don't worry. What happened to us in the past is not good or bad. It simply was what it was. You are just examining what happened and how that impacted your life.

- Remember, you should always be sharing your STORY, whether you are delivering a live presentation or meeting with a new prospect or referral partner.

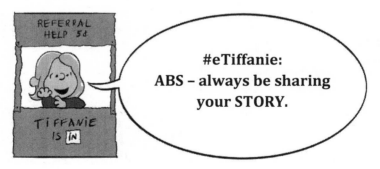

- As you are delivering your STORY, keep in mind that it is not a rehearsed piece of theater. You want to share from the **_heart_**. This is _why you do what you do_. If you come across as snake-oil-salesman slick, you will have a hard time connecting! Be authentic, be you!

In writing this book, I have put what drives me on paper for only the second time in my life. While I memorize most of my keynote presentations word for word (though I do not always follow them when on stage), I have never practiced my story by reading a script and reciting the words. I feel that I want to have my story flow straight from my heart, so, while I do practice my story often, I do not memorize it or read it word for word from a piece of paper.

#eTiffanie: Share your STORY from the heart.

- As you begin to share your STORY, as with everything in life, you will feel awkward. However, each time you share, you will become more comfortable. Just keep your attention on making it emotional and impactful.

- There will be times when you do not feel like sharing your story. In fact, I still have days where I am not sure that I am up for sharing. It could be because people are uncomfortable being open and vulnerable. Those are the times you MOST need to share.

- Depending on how long you have to present, you will need several different length versions: a 30-45 second version (Twitter version), one that is a couple minutes (CliffNotes), and the full version. When networking or doing a short presentation (10 minutes or less), you may want to use your 30-45 second version. When meeting with a prospect for the first time or giving a presentation that is less than an hour, perhaps you can use the CliffNotes version. When you are inspiring a referral partner to refer you more or participating in an extended speaking engagement, you may want to share your full story.

- Practice, practice, practice. Each time you share your story, you will be able to connect more intimately with the reasons you do what you do and eventually dive deeper into your own memories. As with anything new experience, your early attempts may be awkward. This feeling will lessen as you share more.

#eTiffanie: Whether you are in a one-on-one or in front of thousands, start every presentation with WHY you do what you do – your STORY – to help magnetize your audience.

As I mentioned earlier, I have been working with Asentiv® (tampa.asentiv.com) to help thousands of entrepreneurs connect with their story over the past decade. In 2014, the company re-titled the STORY as the Emotionally Charged Connection®. This title perfectly describes exactly how you should approach your STORY: with the goal of creating an emotional connection with your audience!

During the *Ignite your Business* program with Asentiv®, the template used to help focus participants in developing and sharing the *Emotionally Charged Connection®* is:

- **Growing up …**
  Give the audience an overview of what life was like.

- **I remember when (relive the details)…**
  Paint us a picture of a single moment or story. You want the audience to feel like they were there with you.

- **I felt…**
  Use emotions here! If you can describe how you felt with words and feelings that reflect your age at the time these events took place, it will be easier for your audience to connect with you.

- **What I realize today is I help my clients...**
  This is a short statement, typically, that shares exactly how you help your clients, it is the result you create for your client.

- **That's why I do what I do.**

An example:

Growing up, my dad would always come home from work at the mines covered in dirt and grime. **I remember when** he came home, he would always get cleaned up, and dress his best, even if staying at home. **I felt** his pride in always looking good, his best. **What I realize today is I help my clients** look their best with the right clothes and the right marketing, and **that's why I do what I do.**

Once you have your STORY, share it and share it often!

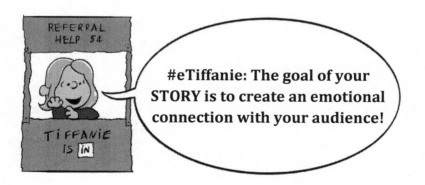

REFERRAL HELP 5¢

TiFFANiE iS IN

#eTiffanie: The goal of your STORY is to create an emotional connection with your audience!

Where and How to Share Your Story

Imagine the following scenario:

*"How often do you do presentations?" Manny asked Sarah.
"I don't do presentations, Manny," Sarah replied with a
frown on her face. "I hate speaking in public."
Manny, with a smirk on his face, asked, "Do you ever do
sales consultations?"
"Of course," said Sarah. "You know that I do sales!"
Manny paused before he spoke, hoping to make an impact
on Sarah. Finally, he countered, "Then you do presentations
all the time."*

The title of this book proposes that you can speak to any
audience, large or small. So far, we've explored the
importance of MAGNETIZING your audience, drawing
them closer and closer to you. You can accomplish this by
sharing your STORY. In this chapter, we are going to dive
into a few options of the different kind of presentations
you can deliver, starting with the one most people
probably imagined when buying this book.

Speaking Engagements

Most of this book will focus on delivering powerful
presentations to a live audience. This could be in front of

10, 100, 1,000, 10,000 or even 100,000 people. The formula and steps will be similar (though there are definitely differences in how you can present for a group of 10 versus 100,000). The tips here will apply more easily to an audience of a dozen or several hundred, though they can be stretched for larger groups. Speaking engagements can include so many different types of organizations, it would take pages and pages to list them all. In every case, though, any presentation you give to a captive audience qualifies as a speaking engagement. Whatever the purpose of your speech, you will want to share your STORY towards the beginning of each presentation, and the longer the presentation, the more details from your STORY you can share throughout. The examples from the previous chapters typically apply to the introductory portion of your presentation. Captivate and magnetize the audience by sharing your STORY as well as speaking with power and passion.

#eTiffanie: Your goal when speaking is to turn a captive audience into an audience that is captivated.

Sales Presentation

You are standing in front of a board room with executives staring back at you. Your PowerPoint slides illuminate the screen behind you, a presentation folder sits in each audience member's hands. Blank and bored expressions cover the faces – this is just another presentation like all the rest.

What if, instead of starting with a dull description of what you do, you start with WHY you do it? This will help you connect with your audience and get them receptive to your pitch. After you share your STORY, you can easily transition to focusing on the BENEFITS. Then, and only then, if they are interested, you can share features. Many times, you will be able to close the sale in less time and with fewer details! Perhaps your intro could include:

Thank you for the opportunity to be here today, to talk about why I think you asked me here, to help your company _____ (benefit here). Is it okay to share with you WHY I am driven to do what I do?

#eTiffanie: A simple introduction that reaffirms the focus of WHAT benefit you are hoping to create, followed by your STORY, can be a great way to start off your sales presentation.

One-on-One

Each time you sit down with a potential prospect or a referral source, you have the opportunity to give a presentation. It may feel completely different from speaking to a large group but your goal remains the same: magnetize the audience.

When you sit down with a prospect for the first time, it is, as always, important for you to lead off with your STORY. This shows who you are and what you believe in. When meeting one-on-one with someone, you can customize the story to that person. Watch for clues from the person you are talking to as you may want to share more or less details.

Whether I am meeting with a prospect or a potential referral source, I like to share what drives me to do what I do so that if they connect with my motives, it encourages them to become a client or pass me referrals more quickly.

Networking

When you network, you often have the opportunity to do mini-presentations. Taking 30 seconds to share your STORY when you are asked "Why do you do what you do?" can be a powerful way to connect. It also offers a way to differentiate yourself from others in your field. Each and every conversation you have while networking is a presentation.

Here is an example of how you could share your story when networking, from Richard Ficca of Florida Coastal

Insurance Agency (floridacoastalinsuranceagency.com):
 "When I was three years old I was attacked by a dog and had my jaw bitten off, requiring extensive surgeries and reconstruction. At the time, I thought that was something that just happened. What I realized, though, is that it was not normal, and it did not have to happen. It helped inspired me to protect people, which is why I became an insurance agent. I have sold insurance for over 20 years to protect my clients so they never have to feel that vulnerable. That's why I do what I do."

Online

I want to acknowledge the rapidly growing world of online presentations, including webinars, hangouts, etc. While the topic as a whole would require an entirely different book and the details would likely be out of date by the time it was published, these are increasingly available presentation options. Just remember, wherever you meet with people, whether online or in person, start with your STORY before almost anything else.

Fundamentally, regardless of the delivery mechanism, the size of your audience, or your location, the approach should remain the same: magnetize your audience!

As we move forward, we will be focusing on presentations done in front of an audience, which mean anything from small groups of three or four people to keynote speeches in front of thousands. While sales presentations and one-on-one talks may be useful, you can easily adapt and apply the skills for group presentations to these specific situations so you can *Knock the Socks off Your Audience.*

Before You Say Yes:
Questions to Ask Before You Accept an Invitation to Present

A personal story from me:

Once upon a time, almost a decade ago, I answered a call from a referral partner. She informed me that she had just found me a speaking engagement. Of course, as I was just beginning to speak in order to help grow my business, I felt excited!

I almost said yes immediately. Luckily, though, I asked a couple of questions, one of which involved the audience. She had a group of retired travelers for me to speak to. I was speechless. After all, my topics are networking and referral marketing. I had no idea what I could possibly talk about with a group that did not need my particular expertise. Thankfully for me, and for the group, I did not accept that engagement.

There are many matters you need to consider when someone is looking to have you speak. While this list is not exhaustive, these are potential questions that you could ask. You will want to choose the most relevant ones for your particular situation.

When first asked to speak:

Why did you ask me to speak?
Leading with this question will help you understand the goals and needs of the person who extended the invitation.

Who is in the audience?
Ensure that the people you want to hear your message will be in the audience. If your topic isn't appropriate for the crowd, then you may want to pass on the request.

How many people do you expect to be in the audience?
Preparing a presentation takes time and effort. This question will help you determine whether all that work is worth it. You may want to drill down a little with this. Ask what that number is based on – can they show you attendance for past events, current ticket sales, or is the estimate just wishful thinking?

How much does this opportunity pay?
Some speaking opportunities will pay, and generously! Many though, at least in your local area, are more likely to be "free" engagements, as the person planning the event will tell you that the opportunity to gain exposure and make connections is payment enough. Occasionally, you may come across an "opportunity" where the speaker has actually had to PAY to be in front of the room, most likely for the "marketing" exposure. There is no right or wrong answer here on whether you should be speaking for FREE versus FEE (though there has been much debate in the

National Speakers Association about it). Just consider which approach works best with your business model.

Will you be covering my travel expenses?
You may be asked to speak outside your local area, and if you are, you will want to inquire into who will be paying for travel expenses.

Can I sell from the stage?
Depending on the event, you may or may not have the opportunity to sell from the front of the room. Typically, though, when a group books me in to speak, I try to minimize pushy sales. Instead, I focus on WOWing people with value and setting myself up for the follow through.

Can I have a Call to Action???
This, to me, is a very important question, especially if I am doing a non-paying event. Your call to action could be as simple as gathering people's information for a follow up, asking permission to add them to your newsletter, or even getting the opportunity for back of the room sales. You will want to ask if you can have a table to put out your "stuff" – literature, business cards, order forms, products, books, etc.

Questions about the presentation itself:

What do you want me to speak on?
This will help you focus your presentation. Do you have a couple of presentations you typically do from which the group can choose? Or would it be best to customize for the group? Getting the coordinator's insight and help on

the best topic for the audience will allow you to walk in with the confidence that you will be sharing the right material with the right people.

How long do I have for the presentation?
Determining how long the presentation is will help you plan and prepare accordingly. Additionally, if the coordinator shares that the presentation will be, for instance, 20 minutes plus a 5 minute Q&A, I recommend requesting no Q&A. My response might be, "Would it be possible for me to do a 25 minute presentation? I can fit additional material in, and I will be happy to remain after the presentation to ensure I answer everyone's questions." Or I ask if I can take questions throughout the presentation, instead of at the end. This helps me ensure that we stay on track with the presentation as well as end on the high note you prepared.

Bonus details:

Are there other speakers at the event?
If yes: *Where am I relative to other presenters?*
Once, I was speaking at a Referral Institute conference, and I learned that I was following the founder of the organization, Dr. Ivan Misner, without a break, AND his topic was how to *Speak Like a Pro*. It was a little nerve-wracking to know that was what I had to follow!
This question also helps you consider how your presentation fits with other presenters' information. I was the third of three speakers at an event, and one of my key points was "why you need to ditch the elevator pitch" (from my first book, *4 ½ Networking Mistakes:*

Maximizing your Networking Efforts by Avoiding Common Mistakes). The first presenter's WHOLE presentation was on how to craft your elevator pitch. It would have been uncomfortable for everyone (the audience, the meeting planner, the other speaker, and I) if I had moved forward and delivered that content. Thankfully, I was able to adjust my presentation accordingly and have a seamless event.

Where am I in the overall program?
This is an important question if you've been invited to a longer event with multiple speakers. Do you speak first thing in the morning? Right before or after lunch? After a break? Closing out the day? You want to be aware of when you will be presenting, and adjust accordingly. Perhaps you might integrate an ice breaker to help get the audience warmed up if you are going first in the morning or craft a lighter presentation if you are following lunch.

What's the structure of the event/meeting?
What is happening during the entire meeting? Do you need to be there for the entire thing or just when you are speaking? Is food being served? Drinks? Will there be networking? This will give you the basic information you need to come prepared for the event.

Event Details:

Who will be introducing me?
Feel free to ask for someone you know that can introduce you with power and passion!

How will the room be set up?
Will the room be in theater style seating, u-shape, or classroom? This may make a difference in your presentation.

What are the audio/video capabilities?
Do they have the equipment for you to deliver a PowerPoint? Will they have a white board or flip chart available? I use PowerPoint in some of my presentations, and it always makes it easier for me if they have the full set-up. Otherwise, I have to bring everything myself. If I am not using the projector, I typically work with a white board to try to engage the audience visually.

Will I have a microphone?
If you are offered a microphone, I ALWAYS recommend that you use it. You may want to ask if it is a handheld microphone or a lapel/lavaliere microphone. If you are not used to presenting with a handheld, practice first with a fake microphone or hairbrush. Personally, I prefer the hands-free option, as I like to talk with my hands. However, not every location has one.

Can I use handouts?
I always recommend some type of handout because a) it gives me the opportunity to get my information into the audience's hands, and b) it helps engage visual and kinesthetic learners. Most likely, you will be allowed to offer handouts. If this is the case, a follow-up question you should ask is whether you need to provide them yourself or if the group will print and distribute the handouts for you.

Can I bring guests?
One of the reasons that some groups like to book me is that I often will bring new people to their events if they are open to the public. I like having people that already know me so that they can speak positively on my behalf, and I can often use them as examples if I do not know many people in the group. If the answer to the guest question is yes, the appropriate follow-ups are, what is the cost for extra guests and how do they register?

Where do I need to be and what time would you like me there?
A meeting planner's worst nightmare is a speaker who doesn't show up. From the planner's perspective, so many things can go wrong. To put their minds at ease, I like to ask exactly where I should go and what time would they like me there. While I am not typically a person who likes to arrive early and wait around, I do prefer to have everything set up before the audience begins to arrive, if possible. If you are meticulous, you may find that this helps put your mind at ease.

Will the audience be eating when I am presenting?
Some speakers I know will not present if food is being served, though I practiced my first words with food on the table! Just be aware that, if food is around, you may be competing for the audience's attention.

Once I was presenting and everyone had box lunches, including sandwiches and Sun Chips. Sun Chips, of course, are infamous for their incredibly noisy bags. Every few seconds throughout the beginning of my presentation, as people were trying to eat, the entire crowd would get distracted by the slow crinkle of the chip bag as people tried in vain to open them without causing a disturbance. After a few failed attempts from the audience, I said something to the effect of, "Okay, who in here is hungry? You have your lunch, but you're afraid to get into those chips because of the noise. So here's what we're going to do. Open your sandwich paper nice and wide, grab those Sun Chips, rip them open, and dump them onto the paper. Then, take the chip bag and toss it into the middle of the table." This got some laughter from around the room. "You can do this in the next 45 seconds, OR you cannot touch your chips for the next 45 minutes." Most of the audience dumped their chips and we were able to move on with the presentation without any further Sun Chip commotion.

As a follow up to asking about food, you may want to ask if they will be serving alcohol during my presentation. If there is, expect even more distractions and maybe even a bit of heckling. In this situation, you are well advised to make the material a little lighter and less in-depth.

Think about the details you may want to know up front before you accept an engagement. Create a checklist or document to help make sure that you have the details you need to be successful.

Making sure you have all the nuts and bolts up front should help you plan and deliver a more appropriate, powerful presentation that will *Knock the Socks off Your Audience*!

Creating a Presentation to Knock the Socks off Your Audience

Imagine yourself sitting in the audience:

"Wow, that was a great introduction!" I thought to myself. I had been waiting for a while to hear this guy speak, and finally, he was here! Then, the very first thing out of his mouth was: "Thank you for being here today. I did not have time to prepare for the presentation, but…"
What??? I'm here, ready to listen, and you start off by saying you didn't prepare. Why did I even bother!

You will almost certainly spend more time preparing for your presentation than you will delivering it and for good reason. It is absolutely crucial that you prepare in advance. You have a very short time to engage the audience, magnetize them, and set them up to have their socks knocked off. To accomplish these goals, you need to carefully structure and word what you have to say in advance.

There is another reason why thorough preparation is necessary: confidence. Think about it. Do you get nervous doing something you've done a thousand times before? Of course not. You drive your car and cook dinner and go about your work without a second thought. You have confidence because you've already experienced success in these areas. You know you can do these things. On the other hand, think of things you've never done in your life. How much confidence would you have doing a guitar solo in front of a hundred people? Well, if you've never touched a guitar in your life, probably none.

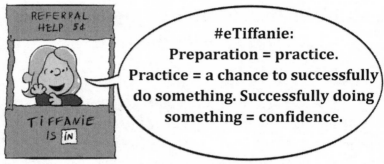

If you want to get up there and knock their socks off, prepare well!

In this section, we will explore:

- What's in the name?
- Writing your Presentation
- Call to Action
- Facts Tell, Stories Sell
- Slide Shows
- Keep the Audience on the Edge of Their Seats
- Use What Your Momma Gave You
- Organizing for the Event

What's in a Name?

At a tradeshow near here:

Anne is reading over the list of presentations for this afternoon's breakout session, and she has three to choose from. Looking down the page, she realizes that she's not familiar with any of the presenters, so she checks out the topics. The first two titles sound average, just the usual same old, same old. The third, though, is intriguing. Her interest is piqued by the title alone. Enough, in fact, that she looks further into the program and picks that option!

Is the name of your presentation important? YES! Absolutely.

Think about it. If titles were not important, then Shakespeare's works would simply be Play No. 1, Play No. 2, Play No. 3, etc. Instead, almost all literary works, music, movies have a memorable title, meant to engage the audience and intrigue people before they're ever premiered.

The goal of titling your presentation is to create anticipation about your topic before they even get into the room. Ultimately, some people will have chosen to be in your audience, or not, simply because of how you named your program.

There may be times when you have a captive audience from inside a group or an organization (meaning they have to go). Still, you want them EXCITED before the presentation starts, rather than dreading the boredom. As a result, no matter the situation, you want a memorable and catchy name that focuses on the benefits of your presentation.

This would be a good time to explore the reasons I chose the names of my own books.

Let's start with this book. Many people are intrigued by the thought of delivering a presentation so powerful that it literally knocks their socks off. There is that... and the fact that most people buying my book may have heard of me before, seen one of my presentations, or followed me online. Which means they know I have a thing for socks.

Now, I did not set out in life to be able to say that I have a fabulous collection of socks, although it's true! I have over 300 pairs of fun and funky socks and my collection keeps growing. In 2015, I started a contest to see how many different pairs of socks I could gather. People began to bring me socks from around the world. The collection continues getting bigger and bigger. You can see some of it on Facebook, perhaps, if you search #TiffaniesSocks. While you're at it, you can follow me at www.facebook.com/tiffaniespeaks. In the end, this title was a marriage of something I like, socks, and a skill I have, delivering presentations.

My first book is another example of how a title can catch people's attention. When I first started writing, my working title was *8 Networking Mistakes*. However, it struck me as boring, and as I continued working on the book, I decided to focus on fewer key ideas. I gave my creative side a little workout and ended up with *4 1/2 Networking Mistakes* (subtitle: *Maximize your Networking Efforts by Avoiding Common Mistakes*). The title creates a little intrigue - I have heard from people who bought the book or come to see the presentation just to learn what the ½ mistake was. Is there a valid reason for the "half" mistake? Yes. It is also great marketing! (Visit Amazon to learn more about *4 1/2 Networking Mistakes* - <u>bit.ly/4halfmistakes</u>)

What comes first, the name or the presentation? They both go hand in hand. I know presenters and authors both who have found success both ways.
Use whichever approach works best for you and your topic!
Begin to magnetize your audience before they even enter the room.

Writing Your Presentation

Whether you have already named your presentation or intend to work that out later, you eventually have to get down to the gritty work of writing. Before you begin, there are critical questions you want to ask for EVERY presentation:

What is the benefit for the audience? What do I want them to get out of the presentation?

By starting with a clear vision of what you want the audience to receive, you will ensure that the presentation will have a clear enough direction to achieve this goal. There are two other things that should remain constant in almost all presentations. First, as we've discussed, you want to start with your STORY. Second, end with some kind of call to action.

When delivering your main idea, I recommend the "Tell 'Em" method. It works like this: you tell them what you are going to tell them, tell them, then tell them what you told them. This will help the audience stay engaged and give them a "Here's where we are going" heads up so they can stay focused. It's like giving them a map. Be aware, though, that you do not have to give away the punch line at the beginning of the story.

#eTiffanie: When presenting, use the "Tell 'Em" method. Tell them what you are going to tell them, tell them, then tell them what you told them.

Before we move on, let's talk about using stories (do note that stories could be success stories, past incidences, fictional happenings used to make a point. These may differ from your STORY or your why). No matter how large or small your audience, you will want to use stories and examples as often as possible, as they make the longest lasting impression! My mentor, Tom Fleming, used to share that presenting is like theater: you always have a beginning, a middle, and an end. Throughout the presentation, there are highs and lows. As a presenter, your job is to tell the story, helping move the audience seamlessly from one conversation to the next. So, your presentation should tell one long, overarching story, but should also be peppered with little anecdotes and examples.

Now it is time to put your ideas into writing. There are several techniques you can use. I will explore a couple in short detail as well as share how I prepare my keynote presentations.

Storyboard:
A very popular technique, storyboarding is like arranging a puzzle. It works by putting key points, stories, exercises, and other relevant information on sticky notes. In preparation, move the sticky notes around until the order flows to your liking. This gives you the outline. Then, when you sit down to write, you simply plug each piece into the right spot to pull it all together.

Bullet/Outline:
Many people start to create their presentation in an outline form. Some people feel that if you don't "script" the presentation, it will come out more naturally. If you are an experienced public speaker, this can work beautifully if you know your material well and have your timing down. However, most may want to approach this technique with caution. I often see it used ineffectively, especially with unpracticed presenters who can easily misspend their time, not leaving enough room to make it through all their points while getting sidetracked rambling on and on about lesser issues. While the bullet method is easier, perhaps, in the writing stage of crafting a presentation, you still need to spend a lot of time practicing to get your time management down. Instead of this format making less practice needed, you will want to practice even more to get the timing right.

Scripted:

I script out my keynote presentations and speeches (although, I do use a slightly different preparation method when facilitating a program). I typically also practice them word for word. This does not mean that I actually deliver it word for word once I get on the stage. Remember, you need to sound natural. So why do it?

I script my presentations word for word for several reasons:

a) Focus and intention. If I am not succinct with my word choice, I have a tendency to ramble, which can lose the audience.

b) I am working on eliminating the "naughty" words. My goal is remain as positive as possible so I try to eliminate as many of the "shouldn't", "wouldn't" and "couldn't" from my presentations.

c) I want to remember the Platinum Rule®
The Platinum Rule (instead of the Golden Rule) says: "Treat others the way *they* want to be treated." There are 4 different behavioral styles, and in Asentiv®'s Room Full of Referrals program (based off the DiSC), these styles are called Go-Getters, Promoters, Nurturers and Examiners. Because the behavioral styles are different, each person has different words that resonate with them.

- Go-Getters are bold, driven people who are always looking for results. I like to use direct words with Go-Getters, such as: confident, results, right, and win.

- Promoters love to have fun and surround themselves with other people doing the same. I like to use upbeat words with Promoters, such as: awesome, enthusiastic, fantastic, and optimistic.
- Nurturers are authentic people who value meaningful relationships. . I like to use comfort words with Nurturers, such as: calm, help, honor, and relate.
- Examiners are reserved and logical people who tend to prefer numbers and analysis. . I like to use concrete words with Examiners, such as: analyze, consistent, effective, and thorough.

For additional information on the four styles, please see Bonus Material: Behavioral Styles or learn more about *Room Full of Referrals* at Tampa.Asentiv.com.

d) And, maybe most importantly – I don't only include words that will resonate with my audience. I also include the "music." By "music," I mean slides, how I use my voice, my body, movement – each of these add to the power of the presentation.

A large part of your success has to do with HOW you deliver the content, not just what you say. Some of the typical "notes" you may see in my presentation include:

- *Pause* – a pause can be a powerful way to bring the audience in before you make an impactful statement OR it can give the members of your audience the time they need to digest the powerful statement that you just shared. A dramatic pause, which should be a full two to three seconds, can quickly capture everyone's attention.

- *Smile* – Facial expressions are so powerful when you are presenting – and the SMILE is the most powerful. You want to remember to smile when appropriate. Also, know you can use a frown, a scowl, wide eyes, or any other facial expression to let everyone know what is happening inside your head.

- *Gesture* – gestures can help the visual audience members truly engage with your story. You want to ensure that you are purposeful with each movement.

  Be natural with your gestures. Think about how you use your hands when talking in an everyday conversation. Amateur presenter's gestures distract the audience and often indicate nervousness, while masterful presenters use them to help put the audience at ease and engage them further.

- *LIGHTENING BOLT* – here I will actually draw out or insert the image of a lightning bolt. What this means to me is that I really need to bring the energy up! I need to get the audience engaged and ready to go.

- *Slide* – when I have a note saying "Slide," it is a reminder that it is time for me to click to the next slide.

  I do not use the slides as a personal reminder of what is coming up next. Instead, the slide should only be a visual re-enforcement of my content for the benefit of my listeners.

Here is an example of part of my script from my keynote presentation from the 4 ½ Networking Mistakes to see the "music" I include:

> Now, I probably should have done this earlier. Now is a good time, though, for m
> DISCLAIMER! If I say something tonight, and you feel like I am directly speaking
> because you have done these things before OR even done them tonight – PLEASE
> NOT pointing at you, saying you did this wrong. **(SMILE)** this is what the experts
> right?
> Run around giving everyone you know a business card.
> **(walk into the audience & pass out cards, including, I don't know you...)**
> And then ask – what are most people going to do with those cards?
> Into the circular file they go!
> The 1st Mistake that even the experts tell you to make?
> I like to call it [slide] "IN PERSON SPAMMING"!
> **(wait for laughs)** I mean, isn't that EXACTLY what we do... not sure if you want
> know us or not... but here we go!

In the end, whichever method works best for your preparation and style, DO IT! Too often people just wing it. While the audience may not be consciously aware that you did not prepare, the consequences will often show in your results.

Preparing in advanced helps to lay a strong foundation to *Knock the Socks off Your Audience.*

#eTiffanie: When you accept a speaking engagement and are putting it into your calendar, be sure that you also schedule prep time so you can organize, write, and practice your presentation.

Call to Action

A presentation is rarely the end of a relationship, at least not ideally. Most often, your goal will be to either create or continue a relationship with the members of the audience. Therefore, you will want to give consideration to your next steps following the speaking engagement.

This means that, for every presentation, you will want to include some sort of call to action. While some groups or companies will invite you in and happily have you promoting and selling from the front of the room, others will prohibit selling. Regardless, you need to offer the audience some way to continue communication with you after the presentation.

You have to ask yourself, after you have determined that selling is appropriate, "What is the next step I want my audience to take?"

If you can't make a direct pitch, ask the audience to try these options instead:

- Trade me a business card for _____ - whether it be your information, a "bonus" from your presentation, adding to your email list, invitation to an upcoming event.

- Text to a specific number to be added to a list (services like KiwiLive).

- Fill out a Tell Me More Sheet (see an example at the end of this chapter).

- Become a client by visiting the back of the room or using order forms on the table for the opportunity to purchase products/services.

- Create an introduction on your behalf, either to a potential prospect or a potential referral source.

- Connect on social media, including promoting the event you are speaking at (usually using hash tags).

Always be sure to have a strong call to action to continue the relationship between you and the audience.

REFERRAL HELP 5¢

TiFFANiE IS [IN]

#etiffanie: A presentation is an opportunity to create or continue a relationship. A next step will be needed.

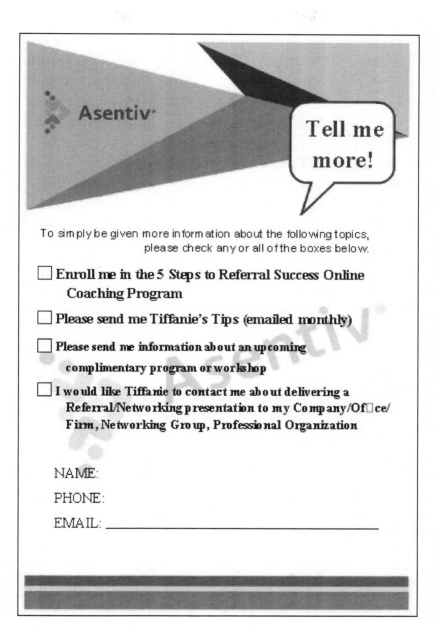

To simply be given more information about the following topics, please check any or all of the boxes below.

☐ **Enroll me in the 5 Steps to Referral Success Online Coaching Program**

☐ **Please send me Tiffanie's Tips (emailed monthly)**

☐ **Please send me information about an upcoming complimentary program or workshop**

☐ **I would like Tiffanie to contact me about delivering a Referral/Networking presentation to my Company/Of☐ce/ Firm, Networking Group, Professional Organization**

NAME:

PHONE:

EMAIL: _____

Facts Tell, Stories Sell

Imagine yourself sitting in the audience:

Yet another pie chart appeared on the screen. It was the fifteenth graphic in as many minutes. I could barely remember the last slide, and I certainly couldn't remember the fourteen other technical details that came before it. I figure I will just take a photo with my camera... I know I'll probably never actually do anything with it. Maybe I should just check my emails instead... this has to be over soon!

It can be very tempting to just rely on facts, details, and statistics to make your case to the audience. After all, if they are true, they will convince people, right? It is true that details can be powerful when used correctly.

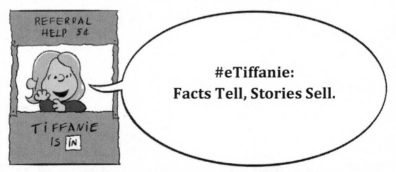

Any time you can use a story to help make a point, people are more likely to remember it. While they may not recall every detail, they will likely remember how they felt. The fact is that most people have an excellent emotional memory but few find that filing information into their brains is easy or interesting. Think about growing up – what do you remember about school? Your friendships and experiences or all the obscure names and dates you crammed for some random history test?

Stories are to your mind what seasoning is to your food. The nutrition may be in the facts, but nobody will want to swallow them if they are bland and flavorless. As often as possible, wrap the audience in a good story, then let that story guide them to the details!

This will help us remember you, and your point, much longer.

Slide Shows

Imagine yourself as Suzy, sitting in the audience:

Suzy sat in the back of the audience, watching the speaker's butt as he read off the screen. The font, in contrast to his backside, was tiny. She found it unreadable from her seat. The last 28 minutes had felt like 28 hours, and, according the agenda, she still had 32 minutes of this drivel to suffer through. "Everything he has said has come off the slide, and he hasn't looked back at the audience in 17 minutes, except when a guy sneezed. You would have thought the guy sneezed on purpose the way that the presenter glared at him. Why, oh why, am I putting myself though this torture? I think now would be a good time to go to the bathroom."

Having an electronic visual during your presentation, most commonly in the form of a slide show or PowerPoint, is supposed to help engage the audience on a visual level, giving you the opportunity to support your words with pictures, sounds and video.

Too often, though, speakers will use the PowerPoint as a crutch, putting all their words on a slide and sometimes even just reading directly off it!

The purpose of a slideshow is to ENHANCE your presentation, not deliver it for you.

Therefore, when it comes to your slides, the fewer words, the better! Slides with 3, 4, even 10 bullet points contain too much! If you need to provide that level of detail, here are a few fixes:

a) have each bullet be only a single word

b) make each bullet point a slide

c) hand out a worksheet with the written details

I really prefer to combine slides and handouts. If you have a paragraph of important detail you want to share, please do not make the audience stop to write it out or grab their phone to take a photo. Put it in writing on a worksheet or send them to a page on your website where they can get the information.

It is true that many people will request slide printouts from speakers. I also know some presenters who will offer slides to the audience. However, to me, the best speakers typically design slides that simply accent the presentation rather than delivering all of the information in a wall of words!

There is so much more that can be said about creating powerful visuals to accent your presentation, a whole other book's worth, in fact! Luckily, you do not have to wait for me to write it, as Garr Reynolds has already done that in *Presentation Zen*. I highly recommend you pick up a copy if you need to do slideshow presentations often.

#eTiffanie: Your slides should enhance your presentation!

Keep the Audience on the Edge of Their Seats

When you give a live presentation, your job goes beyond simply delivering content. You also have to keep the audience engaged. So, why include a chapter on engagement in the preparation section of this book? Because the techniques you use to get your audience's attention will determine how you write your presentation.

There are a variety of ways you can keep the audience engaged. Sharing your story early on in your presentation should help pull the audience in early. To keep the audience in tune through the rest of your presentation, you will want to consider including physical movement, asking questions, and using humor. Of course, you cannot use every technique on this list at the same time. Rather, think of these options as a menu from which you can pick the methods that resonate best with you and that suit your topic and situation.

- *Asking questions:* You can ask questions to help engage the audience, either by requesting specific replies from people or just asking for a show of hands in response to simple yes/no questions. Even rhetorical questions can keep people's attention on the topic – it's hard not to answer one in your own mind.

- *Group exercises:* Group exercises can be a powerful way to help the audience bond with each other, while giving both them and the speaker a brief break from the one-directional focus of a typical speech. Pick appropriate exercises for your topic and your audience. For example, an ice breaker at the beginning of a presentation will help everyone relax while drawing them closer to each other and your topic.

- *Using Names:* If possible, using the names of people in the audience can increase the level of engagement. You can also use shared or familiar topics that everyone relates to, such as the city, profession, hobbies, particular company employees, etc.

- *Quiet Time:* Sometimes, something as simple as letting the audience take a few moments to work through what you have shared can be powerful. This approach also increases the likelihood that they will implement your ideas by getting right to work on them.

- *Humor:* Make the audience laugh! Even tickling their funny bone just a little can help them stay tuned in. Know that there are different kinds and levels of humor, and you don't need every joke to have people rolling on the floor with tears streaming from the eyes. A few well-placed chuckles are enough to keep everyone engaged.

- *Video:* If used correctly, videos can give the audience the opportunity to get information from someone else while you get a quick break. Videos also change the flow of a presentation. This variety keeps everything from getting too repetitive.

- *Images & Props:* These critical components help engage visual learners and make your concepts more memorable.

- *Worksheets*: Utilizing worksheets keeps everyone involved because the audience needs to listen closely for the cues they need to write things down. Written work also activates different parts of the brain.

When deciding which techniques you will use to engage your audience, be aware that there are three basic learning styles and that each person has one that is dominant. When you speak to each style, you will ensure that you are reaching everyone.

Auditory learners need to hear the information. Good methods for communicating with auditory learners include:

- Using the "Tell 'Em" method of storytelling

- Asking questions

- Sparking a conversation between yourself and the audience

Kinesthetic learners need to be physically involved when learning. At the very least, they learn well with movement, note taking and highlighting, even doodling.

Good methods for communicating with kinesthetic learners include:

- Giving them handouts so they can take notes

- Getting everyone up and moving around! Allow for role playing if possible

- Playing music and giving appropriate breaks to help "move" the audience

Visual learners need to see the information. Good methods for communicating with visual learners include:

- Including visual stimulants, such as slides, whiteboard drawings, or flip charts

- Using charts, graphs, cartoons, and pictures

- Giving them bright, visually interesting handouts with margins for note taking

Powerful presenters work to engage all three styles in their presentations to help keep the entire audience fully engaged!

These are just a few ways that you can engage the audience. If you look through them closely, you will find a common thread: activation! People learn best, understand how topics relate to them, and get the most enjoyment through real experience and participation. The more you make listeners feel like they are partners and participants in your presentation, the more engaged they will be. And the more engaged they are, the greater the chance your message (including your STORY) will land, and stay, with impact!

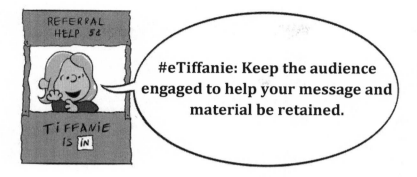

Use What Your Momma Gave You

Ferris Bueller's Day Off came out while I was growing up, and I have a vivid memory of the scene where the teacher, Ben Stein, was droning on about Economics while the students in the classroom sat there with glazed, vacant expressions on their faces.

Unfortunately, we can all relate.

We have all seen the presentations like this: boring. They drive the audience to the point of sleep or tears, or, even worse with today's technology, to simply pull out their smart phones while their minds leave the room.

There are several ways that you can help add some pizzazz to your presentation, which can help keep the audience in tune with your message. Thankfully, you already have many of the tools you need to accomplish this, and they are ones that your momma gave you – your voice and your body.

While what you say is important, so is **how** you say it. A great presentation is more than just a river of words coming out of your mouth.

Early on in life, perhaps as young as kindergarten, teachers were instructing us on how to listen to their verbal cues. They gave these frequently and often, cluing us in to which items would be "on the test."

How did they do this?

- *Repetition*: When you want a point to stick in your audience's mind, I recommend repeating it several times. As you come back to the same phrase two, three, or four times, you will notice more and more audience members writing down your words.

- *Stress*: Add emphasis to words and phrases that you want the audience to make a note of. This comes across the same as saying, "Pay attention, this will be on the test".

- *Pregnant Pause*: By pausing before or after an idea, you signify to the audience that something very important is coming. Additionally, you can use a speaking phrase I have heard, ***"Let it Land."*** This technique works by pausing for a full three seconds, truly letting the content you just shared sink in.

When it comes to your voice, *variety is the spice of life*! If you think about how you carry on regular conversations, your voice shifts naturally from one idea to the next. Likewise, you will want to use vocal variety to help keep everyone tuned in to your frequency. Consider varying your...

- *Volume:* Monotone sounds put people to sleep, so raise and lower your volume to keep the audience on their toes.
Amateur speakers occasionally think that to really make a point, they need to almost YELL! In reality,

the opposite is often true. If you really want to pull the audience in, lower your voice to deliver the killer point (though be careful not to speak so softly that the audience cannot hear you).

- *Speed:* during your presentation you will want to speed up some times and slow down at others. Sticking to one speed means you will start droning almost right away. If you keep a slow pace throughout, you can easily put the audience to sleep, while going 90 miles an hour the entire time makes it hard for them to stay focused. Let your speed fluctuate, all the while enunciating clearly to help the audience hear and retain your message.

- *Pitch:* adds natural movement, even within a single sentence. Much like speed, using only one pitch will make you sound like a whirring ceiling fan after a while. Just keep it conversational. Using a higher pitch at the end of yes/no questions is typical, while statements usually end on a lower pitch.

- *Tone:* this is the emotion you want to add to the words, the energy in your voice. Tone is especially important when you share the story of WHY you do what you do – it's the key to making your stories believable!

When it comes to your voice, by all means embrace what makes you different! Don't worry about that accent. New accents can help engage the audience's ears, and different can be appealing as long as everyone understands what you are saying.

For example, I have a noticeable Southern accent (well, I think it's normal). Others point it out as Southern). While I try to ensure that I speak clearly, I also wish to embrace my heritage, I often let my audience know early on about my Southern background and give them this translation:

A Quick Guide to Southern Grammar
ain't = isn't
y'all = you all

Tiffanie Kellog
#eTiffanie

I believe embracing who you are does help build your authenticity and makes you human. You need to convey both to deliver a successful speech. Besides, this slide typically gets a chuckle!

In addition to using your voice, body language is critical for getting your ideas across with non-verbal cues. One of the most powerful things you can do when speaking is SMILE! As recommended earlier, you want to deliver your presentation with power and passion. It is very important to look like you are having a good time if you want the audience to feel the same. Smiling throughout the entire presentation is not necessary (and might come off as creepy). Use your smile at important, appropriate junctures, and remember you have a myriad of additional facial expressions that you can use to assist in making your point.

While we're on the topic of your face, maybe you recall the saying: "The eyes are the window to the soul." Use your eye contact to help you connect better with the audience!

Movement can also be powerful in helping keep things fresh for the audience. If possible move around the room. If you have a mic stand and can't walk around, at least gesture with your arms.

There is an important benefit for your audience that comes when you physically move around the room. It requires them to move their eyes, head, and neck as well, giving them an opportunity to loosen up while you pull them along with you. You might simple walk into the audience or just pace from one side of the stage to the other. The only trap to avoid is rocking back and forth from one foot to another. You don't want to make your people seasick by watching you. When presenting, always stand strong and tall!

Additionally, at times, you can use movement by calling on your spectators to move themselves, possibly by raising their hands, standing, or letting them take a stretch break, which can help everyone clear their minds and come back to listen feeling refreshed.

Gestures are another way that you can use your body to keep your presentation fresh! Be aware of how you use them, though – move with purpose, not as a random release of nervous energy. The people watching you can tell the difference. You also don't want to stand completely still.

To get a feel for how to use gestures naturally, I recommend that you take note on how you move your hands in normal conversations. The gestures you use during your presentation should mimic your normal motion.

The best time to gesture is when you need to help move a story along. For example, hold up three fingers when you share "three points I will be making today...." This will resonate well with the visual people in your audience.

You were born with a voice, a body, and hands, so treat them as the tools they are. By using what your momma gave you, you will be able to give the most to your audience. You can add variety to your presentations, help everyone retain more information, and get the audience to like you. Everyone likes a speaker who isn't boring! Now...

Knock their socks off!

#eTiffanie: Use what your momma gave you, your body and voice, to help keep the audience engaged when you speak.

Organizing for the Event

One key part of your presentation actually has nothing to do with anything you will do on stage. Think about it. If your audience has never heard of you before, why would they listen to you? And if they like what you have to say, will they have the tools to follow up with you later? You don't want to rely on their note-taking to ensure that they know how to contact you or even remember your name, so you need to prepare everything they may need and get it into their hands well before they listen to you speak.

Thankfully, good event planners have thought of this and will likely request the relevant information well in advance. This chapter covers all the things you will probably need to deliver to them to help your presentation run professionally and smoothly.

The first items you may need, after you sign the contract, are going to be a presentation description and your headshot. Therefore, as you are creating your presentations, it's a good idea to create a brief description of what your presentation is about in addition to your title. You want to sell your concept with your description because your goal is to generate excitement about the presentation before it even begins! Instead of simply stating the content, share how your audience can benefit from the program. When you are asked for the description, write it out and share it with the event organizer. Then, be sure to save a file for yourself so you can reuse it for the next engagement.

Professional speakers need professional headshots, which means that it should be recent and actually look like you. People frequently tell me that I look just like my picture. In my head, I am thinking, "Of course I do! That's what a picture is for." The fact that so many people share this with me makes me think that a lot of people don't have pictures that represent them well. So, if you don't have a high-quality picture, get one.
There are options you can use, whether a headshot, a picture of you speaking, or if you have a "thing", for example my photo showing my socks.

The next thing to prepare will be your bio. The event organizer will likely need this to use on the event website and promotional flyer. The bio is your best opportunity to begin building credibility before the actual event. Give consideration to what you want the audience to know about you, and again, save this material!

Personally, I keep a regularly updated document that has my bio, program descriptions, and several introductions. This makes it easy to ensure that the people who have booked me to speak have the tools they need to promote me.

Finally, something that event organizers want more and more frequently these days is a video with which to promote the event. These don't need to be long or professionally done. Typically, you can use a quick 30 second video you shot in your office. These can be excellent promotional tools for event websites, social media, or an email blast.

If you can give your event organizers good material, you will make it easier for them to promote you. By doing this, you will make it more likely that they will extend future invitations for you to speak.

Sample Promotions for my Presentations

<u>4 ½ Networking Mistakes</u>

Do you network to help you gain referrals?
Would you like your networking to be easier, more effective, and even more fun?

If your answer is YES, you will want to attend the *4 ½ Networking Mistakes* presentation to discover a better way to network! During this program, we will explore:

- Why you may not want to pass out business cards when networking
- Why your name tag may be hurting – instead of helping – at events
- Why you should never use your elevator pitch when meeting new people
- Why networking alone won't help you grow your business
- The half mistake!

Join us for these tips, and more, as we discuss *4 1/2 Networking Mistakes,* mistakes even the experts make. Referral expert Tiffanie Kellog will help you turn networking from an ineffective chore to a fun, potent tool for success!

<u>5 Steps to Referral Success</u>

Growing your business by referral is not easy, but it can be SIMPLE if you know the 5 Steps to Referral Success!

During this program with Tiffanie Kellog, we will explore:
- Who can be passing you MORE referrals?

- What you can do right now to make it easier for people to pass you referrals
- How to develop stronger relationships with the people in your network, inspiring them to send more business your way
- The best, most effective techniques for requesting referrals

Join us for the answers to these questions and more during the *5 Steps to Referral Success*!

Networking and Communicating with Ease

Ever wonder why a few people are awesome, others are amazing, but many are just plain awkward?

In the *Networking and Communicating with Ease* program, we explore the motivations behind human behavior so that **you can adapt to others** and make your referral conversations more effective, more rewarding, more productive, and YES, even more FUN!!

With this knowledge, you'll be able to modify your communication style to quickly establish rapport and trust with nearly anyone. Applying these concepts will help you become a master networker as you discover how leveraging behavioral styles will make your networking pay off in tangible business results.

Sample Bios for my Presentations

Short Version:

Over the past decade, Tiffanie Kellog has helped thousands of entrepreneurs grow their businesses by creating referrals for life.

As the author of *4 1/2 Networking Mistakes: Maximize your Networking Efforts by Avoiding Common Mistakes*, Tiffanie is in demand as a professional keynote speaker, coach and facilitator with Asentiv® and is co-owner of a business with her husband Rob.

"Growing a business by referrals is a dream for many entrepreneurs," says Tiffanie. "My goal is to help them achieve their dreams by giving them the tools they need to make more money in less time, so they can have more fun."

All work and no play would make Tiffanie a dull girl, so, in addition to helping people build their own spectacular lives, she enjoys her passion for "nerdy" hobbies, craft beer, and fundraising to help fight cancer.

Shortest Version:

Tiffanie Kellog is the author of *4 1/2 Networking Mistakes: Maximize your Networking Efforts by Avoiding Common Mistakes*, a professional keynote speaker, coach, and facilitator with Asentiv®.

Tiffanie says, "Growing a business by referrals is a dream for many entrepreneurs. My goal is to help them achieve their dreams by giving them the tools they need to make more money in less time."

Longer Version:

Tiffanie Kellog is the author of *4 ½ Networking*

Mistakes: Maximize your Networking Efforts by Avoiding Common Mistakes, a cutting-edge guide to avoiding the gaffes that even experts tell you to make.

She entered the entrepreneurial world in 2003 and quickly discovered that referrals and networking were the most powerful approaches to growing her business. In 2006, she began sharing her system for success, and, since then, has shared her knowledge with thousands of professionals across the country helping them grow their businesses and make more money.

With Tiffanie's insights, instead of an epiphany, people get to experience an "eTiffanie," a new way of looking at growth that helps entrepreneurs increase their profit while saving time. Because of her innovative approach and engaging speaking style, she has been recognized by the *Tampa Bay Business Journal* as one of the top business speakers in the Tampa Bay area!

In all she does, Tiffanie is committed to helping revolutionize the way business owners and entrepreneurs think about marketing. "Growing a business by referrals is a dream for many entrepreneurs," says Tiffanie. "My goal is to help them achieve their dreams by giving them the tools they need to make more money in less time, so they can have more fun."

Before Your Presentation

Have you ever been in a similar situation to Adam?

Adam awoke with a jolt, his body covered in sweat. The nightmare that had been plaguing him for the past few weeks had returned. In his dream, he had shown up to the biggest presentation of his career unprepared. He forgot the whole thing and didn't have his slides, worksheet, or PANTS!!! This was too much. Everyone was noticing the bags under his eyes as his sleep quality got worse and worse. "Maybe I should start getting ready", Adam thought. "Perhaps that will help the nightmares stay away!"

After creating your powerful presentation and learning how to magnetize a crowd so that you can *Knock the Socks off Your Audience*, there are a few things you will want to do to ensure that you will be ready to stroll up to the stage with absolute confidence.

This section includes:

- Practice (and Practice and Practice Some More)
- Dress to Impress
- What to Bring with You
- Your Introduction
- How to Master Nervousness and Stage Fright
- What Could Go Wrong?

Practice
(and Practice and Practice Some More)

You have scripted your presentation. You carefully chose every word. You thought long and hard about your body language. You are ready. Right? Not if you haven't practiced!

If you want to give an outstanding presentation, you should actually spend more time **practicing** than you do creating. While content is key, and what you have to say is *muy importante*, your words will never sink in without a *powerful* delivery.

In the next chapter, we are going to explore some tried and true practice techniques – the same ones I use myself.

How do I know they work? Because when I complete my presentations, people often let me know how "effortless" everything looked, how "natural" it seemed – like I was having a "conversation." While I am a master of the material I present, practicing plays a large part in the fluid effortlessness that comes across on stage.

Practice, Practice, Practice

By repeatedly practicing your presentation, you will become deeply familiar with the tiniest details of your content, allowing your speech to flow more naturally. This happens because you will likely discover in your practice sessions that some words or phrases do not function together well. You will also notice sections that trip you up and have a chance to get your timing down.

Another benefit of repetitive practice is experience. Each time you practice, you become more comfortable delivering the content. By the time you get in front of the room, it will practically be second nature to you. As a result, you will be able to focus on speaking with power, passion, and confidence – the true qualities that compel people to like you!

Dr. Ivan Misner, the father of modern networking and a popular keynote speaker, believes that you should practice at least 4-6 times before delivering a presentation to a live audience for the first time. For me, the more important the presentation is to me, the more times I will practice. Some presentations I have done include practicing dozens of times, including reciting my presentation over and over again out loud as I drive around town.

Perfect Practice Makes Perfect

The old saying goes – "Practice Makes Perfect." The problem is that, however we practice, we are preparing to deliver it in exactly that the way. What if your practice includes bad habits and mistakes? You do not want to ingrain those! Instead, you want to practice your presentation as if you were delivering it, each and every time.

For me, this includes always practicing while standing up and, also, while moving around. I do not speak in one spot or sitting down or in front of a computer. Therefore, when you practice, get up on your feet! Choose an open area in your house where you can move about unencumbered. Are you using slides? Then set up your computer and click through them just as you intend to do in real life. Make sure to practice your wording as well as the "music" we discussed previously (like using the clicker to advance my slides, smiling, and gesturing).

Practice with an Audience

You have two options here. If you have a live audience to work with, maybe friends or family, take advantage of that opportunity! If you don't, you can always use yourself as an audience using the tips below.

- In front of a live audience:

    If there are people in your life whom you know, trust and are willing to offer you valid and constructive feedback, ask if you can practice your presentation in front of them. People in your office, friends, and family can all help give you the opportunity to get feedback as well as giving yourself a chance to deliver in a realistic situation.

There is one trap you need to avoid, however. As an example, I have a grandmother who loves everything that I do. While this is great for my ego, her feedback does not help me get better. Be sure that the people you ask for help can give you honest, constructive feedback, and be willing to take it.

Anyone can be an audience member. I have a family of Maltese who have seen a great number of my presentations. My goal, when presenting to my dogs (without any treats in my pockets) is that if I can keep them engaged for 10, 20, or 30 minutes while they cannot understand a word, then I should be good with a human audience! (If I were delivering this presentation live, I would pause for several seconds to let the concept land and hopefully get a laugh out of the audience.)

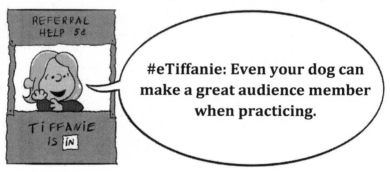

#eTiffanie: Even your dog can make a great audience member when practicing.

- In front of yourself
    - *Video:* Watching yourself do a presentation can be very powerful, though not everyone likes to watch themselves on video. For whatever reason, sometimes when people

watch themselves for the first time (or any time, for that matter), they feel uncomfortable with what they see. Personally, I have hundreds of videos uploaded on YouTube for the public, in addition to many videos I have taken just for myself. I still do not like seeing myself on video, I watch them anyway.
Some of my largest strides as a speaker have come from watching myself on video. I have picked up on nervous habits (playing with my hair and wedding ring) and noticed words that I used too frequently.

o   *Mirror:* Delivering a presentation in front of a mirror (or a selfie screen on a computer) will give you immediate feedback on what you are doing, and you will quickly be able to make corrections. However, unless you have a very large mirror, you will be limited to a small area where it will be difficult to walk around.

Time yourself

So many great presentations get derailed because speakers do not properly measure the time they need for each point. If you want to avoid the embarrassment of running too long or too short, you must practice your timing. As you are practicing, be aware that most people fit into 1 of 3 of the following categories:

1) Some people tend to speak more quickly when they present in front of an audience. You may do so because of nerves or you may just speak more quickly when "on-stage," but you need to be aware so you can practice speaking more slowly or filling the time differently.

   As you present more and more often, (which I assume you are doing because you are reading this book), you will see how "short" you typically run. If this is a persistent issue, you can prepare additional content to deliver in case you find yourself with extra time at the end.

#eTiffanie: Close with power and passion. Do not open your presentation to questions at the end, as often the questions can derail your momentum. Instead

2) Some people practice and deliver it in the same time frame. I am extremely jealous of people that fall into this category. If you are one of the lucky ones, keep up the good work!

3) Others practice and then go long. Personally, I fall into this category. I know that however long it takes me to get through a practice speech, I will typically use 20-25% more time when on stage. If

this is true for you as well, give yourself a shorter script to work from.

Do you need to spend a LOT of time practicing? Absolutely.

As you get better at presenting and start reusing presentations, you won't need to practice as often as you repeat presentations.

Until that time though, I recommend that you PRACTICE, PRACTICE, PRACTICE!

Even I still practice over and over again!

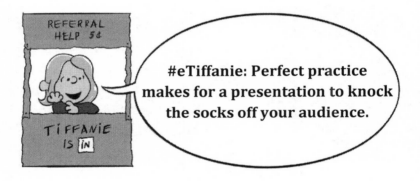

#eTiffanie: Perfect practice makes for a presentation to knock the socks off your audience.

If you want additional help in practicing your presentations, you may want to visit a local chapter of Toastmasters. This organization helps many people develop their speaking skills. Find a chapter near you at www.toastmasters.org.

Dress to Impress

I was sitting in the audience at a local networking meeting in 2010, watching a person I knew well give a presentation. She had been excited about it and had spent the past month prepping and practicing. The day before, she decided she was going to go shopping for a new look. She wanted to feel great.

Unfortunately, from the minute she stepped on stage, she looked awkward. She had an amazing pair of shoes on her feet, yet they seemed to be making it hard for her to walk. And, apparently, someone had convinced her to buy Spanx! She ended up tugging on her undergarments every couple of minutes.

Her awkward gait and fidgeting were distracting to me. I wonder if they were to anyone else in the audience.

No matter how good your presentation is, you always want to look good – your best, in fact – when you are on stage! Start out on the right foot with the audience by looking the part. If you want people to like you based on your message, don't give them a reason to dismiss you before you have even started to speak.

#eTiffanie: When you are
stepping in front of the audience,
you want to impress.
Start with the way you dress!

What should you consider wearing when getting ready to speak to a big group? For that matter, what should you consider wearing in any public setting?

Many sources recommend dressing better than your audience, though perhaps only by a little. You do not want to be overdressed (unless wearing a tuxedo is a part of your brand) but you definitely do not want to dress more casually than your clients.

Here's what I typically advise my own clients to do:

#eTiffanie: When you present,
dress as if you were meeting with
the best potential prospect.

You want to be impressive though also authentic. You do not want to be someone other than yourself when you step up on stage. You just want to be the sharpest, best-looking version of you! Find your best colors and get advice from someone with a good eye if fashion isn't your cup of tea. Do find a style that matches your personality. For example, if you never wear skirts, don't wear them for a presentation. Your discomfort will affect your stage presence.

On the other hand, what if you are typically a t-shirt and shorts type of person, or someone who always wear flip-flops? Remember that while you are training to be yourself, you are being your professional self - you represent your business.

Pay attention to trends, as well. Is your look from this decade? Or, preferably, from within the past couple of years? If you look out of date, your audience may conclude that your ideas are behind the times as well. Need help looking your best? Consider working with a stylist to help you find the right fashion for you.

Some may think that what you wear is unimportant, fashion being trivial. Even if you believe that, know that your clothing and your appearance does impact your first impression. So does personal grooming. Does your haircut still look fresh or are you overdue? Do you need to shave? Is a visit to a salon necessary – perhaps you need help with nose hair, chin hair, ear hair? Especially if the session is being recorded and projected on a wide screen, you need to ensure that you are well put together. Have someone double check you for any stray hairs, messy clothes, or other distractions before you step on stage.

Even accessories need your attention, as they can be distractions that you may want to eliminate. You may choose to empty your pockets of keys and loose change, remove your cell phone from your belt, and make sure that any jewelry is not noisy or distracting.

Remember, fidgeting is also distracting. You should be able to move around easily, so go for something that is not too tight or too loose. Does your outfit fit correctly, or is it in need of some tailoring if you have gained or lost weight recently? Consider your shoes, too. If you do not know how to walk in high heels, ladies, you may not want to wear them for your presentation. You want your focus to be on delivering your powerful presentation, not on getting comfortable or trying to keep your balance.

Finally, a note for women (and a few men): because you will be on stage, you will want to wear heavier make up than usual, especially when lighting and cameras are involved.

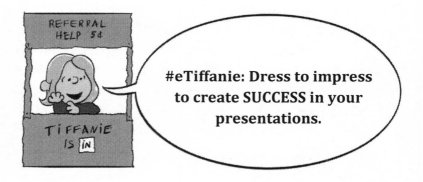

What to Bring with You

Could this ever happen to you?

"Glad you are here, Thomas," said the event organizer. "Do you have a thumb drive with your presentation on it?"
"I emailed that over last week," Thomas said.
"Well, we had some technical issues, and do not have your presentation or your bio. I was hoping you had an extra with you? Hopefully?" prayed the event organizer.
Thomas replied...

Hopefully, if you were in this situation you would be prepared. As a speaker, being prepared goes beyond practicing and dressing the part, you want to make sure that you have with you anything and everything you may need!

To ensure that you have all the tools you will need, it is a good idea to put together a checklist of what you should bring each and every time you present. This chapter will give you the building blocks for your checklist. Feel free to add more to suit your specific needs.

In alphabetical order:

- *Banners/Signs* – if you have a banner to highlight yourself or your company, set it up behind you on stage to reinforce your brand, or place it by a table where people can find you before and after the engagement.

- *Bio* – Be sure you have your powerful introduction.

- *Business cards* – While you may have your contact information on your worksheets and handouts, many people still like having business cards. If you have any other collateral material, like brochures, catalogs, price sheets, etc., bring those too.

- *Camera & tripod* – This is a must have on my list. Whether you want to capture testimonials after the program or just get yourself on film, this is a handy way to document what you do.

- *Directions* – If you are driving, you may want printed directions to the event in the unlikelihood that you have technical issues with your GPS or phone.

- *Evaluation form* – Some speakers use an evaluation form (with permission of the event coordinator) to gather feedback from the audience on how the presentation went and additional presentations the audience might want to hear from the speaker, as well as testimonials.

- *Flip chart/whiteboard + markers* – To help engage the visual learners in the room, you may want to bring your own flip chart or have the meeting provide one for you.

- *Handouts* – If you, not the event planner, are supplying your own handouts, then be sure to bring plenty! You may wish to have a paper master copy in case you need copies made, or the electronic file if you need to print additional copies.

- *Honey and/or cough drops* – In case you have a coughing spell or sore throat, cough drops or honey can be helpful.

- *Meeting planner or host's cell number* – In case you get lost, need last minute directions, are stuck in traffic, or need advice on where to park.

- *Name tag* – When you have the opportunity to network, your face plus your name tag will hopefully spark recognition from the people at the event - "Oh, you're our speaker today."

- *Notes or outline of your presentation* – Even if you have memorized your presentation, bring a copy of your notes or outline, just in case.

- *Pens* – Pens with your information or website on them can make a great giveaway that makes it easy for the audience to follow up with you.

- *Products to sell* – If you have physical products to sell or purchase order forms, I recommend bringing those with you (Supplies could include books, workbooks, enrollment forms for clients, products, and even physical merchandise.). When people are ready to purchase, you want to make it easy for them. You may wish to include a way to take credit card payments on your list.

- [ ] *Props* – Do you have visuals that can help share your message? Bring them!
  (For example, during my keynote, 4 ½ Networking Mistakes, I talk about people passing out unwanted business cards that often end up in the trashcan. When I make this point, I actually have people put the cards I just handed them into a trashcan that I bring with me.)

- [ ] *Technology* – This includes your computer, a projector (cables, screen), a clicker, and perhaps an extension cord or power cord. Also, always bring a backup USB if the group that booked you is using a computer already and you are simply plugging in your presentation. Remember that, when technology is involved, you may want a back up for your back up!

- [ ] *"Tell Me More" sheets* – This is a simple form that lets the audience ask for more information. Some options could include: a free follow-up consultation call, a subscription to a newsletter, an invitation to an additional program, or a free follow-up such as an ebook, white paper, or online program. (Recall the example from the earlier chapter on your call to action)

- [ ] *Timer* – Do you use a timer, or even your watch? Maybe another person helps you keep time? However you want to do it, be sure you have a time management tool so your speech doesn't run long.

☐ *Travel documents* – If your presentation is outside your local area, you may need your plane tickets, hotel reservations, passport, etc. While many people keep some of this information electronically, it is always a good idea to have a backup copy.

You may have additional things you want to bring with you depending on the topic or situation, so make a customized checklist before each engagement. You do not want to get there and discover that you are missing a critical piece!

813-263-9690 www.TiffanieKellog.com referrals@tiffaniekellog.com

Checklist for Speaking

- ☐ Handouts
- ☐ Power Point Outline or Presentation notes
- ☐ Tell me more sheets
- ☐ Enrollment forms (for upcoming programs)
- ☐ Bio
- ☐ Meeting planner or host's cell number
- ☐ Banners
- ☐ Books
- ☐ Business cards
- ☐ Camera & tripod
- ☐ Cough drops
- ☐ Name tag
- ☐ Pens
- ☐ Speaker Sheet

Optional
- ☐ Computer
- ☐ Projector
- ☐ Speakers
- ☐ Power Cord
- ☐ Projector Screen
- ☐ Whiteboard & Markers
- ☐ Props
  - ☐ 4 ½ Networking Mistakes: Trash Can, Checkbook, Stack of Business Cards
- ☐ Otro

Your Introduction

In 2014:

I was standing off-stage, waiting for my introduction. However, the person that I had coached before the event to introduce me was nowhere to be see, and another woman was reading my bio. As she read, she mispronounced eTiffanie. I cringed, but what could I do at that point? Then, to my horror, she proceeded to read the note for the person doing my introduction – "Reader – read "eTiffanies" - it is said almost like epiphanies, but with Tiffanie." *She then looked at me like I was crazy for having written that into the notes. Unfortunately, there was nothing I could do at that point.*

Before you even step on stage, you will want to have a discussion with the person who will introduce you and go over what they will say.

This person is very important. Some organizations have a designated "introducer," so they may or may not know you. If possible try to have someone who knows you fill this role so they can introduce you with power and passion.

Why? Because the introduction is the first opportunity to get the audience to LIKE you! Even if they don't know you, you *always* want to have someone introduce you when you are speaking, even if it just takes a few sentences.

What are "must-haves" in your introduction? There are many different formulas out there for the most powerful introduction. To me, though, it comes down to this question: What do you want your bio to accomplish?

If it's an ice breaker, perhaps you will want to include something silly about yourself. If you aim to build credibility, then you may want to share degrees, awards, certifications, and accomplishments.

You should have physical copies of your bio with you for every engagement, even if you have emailed it in advance. It is also a good idea to print it in a larger than normal font (18-24 font) to make it easier on the person reading it. You can also help your introducer by reviewing any hard-to-pronounce names or words prior to the event.

#eTiffanie: Get your introduction delivered with power and passion, and make the audience like you before you even say a word!

By the way, I have seen two speakers use a professional video for their introduction before. This requires a significant investment of time and money. Most people opt for a written bio that someone reads for them.

Sample Introductions

Here are two introductions that I use at events, depending on the audience and my goals.

Note that in the first introduction, I have a couple notes for my reader in parenthesis to help the delivery.

When I am presenting a version of 4 ½ Networking Mistakes:

Are you looking to grow your business?

And do you network to help you gain referrals?

And, would you like an easier and more effective way to network?

Since you answered yes, you are in the RIGHT PLACE - and be glad that you're here.

Our presenter today is a masterful speaker, talented facilitator, and author of *4 ½ Networking Mistakes.*

She's been sharing referral marketing techniques for almost a decade,

she's a sports car driver (pause)

well, she has a sports car that she drives a lot,

and is responsible for 'eTiffanies' around the world!

(Reader – read "eTiffanies" - it is said almost like epiphanies, but with Tiffanie)

Today, she will be helping us network the ASENTIV® way,

which will help us make more money, save time, and have more FUN!

She's a speaker, a master networker, and an Eager Beaver!

It's my pleasure to introduce Tiffanie Kellog.

Please turn your attention to the screen!

<u>Generic:</u>

Today I have the honor to introduce you to Tiffanie Kellog.

As author of *4 ½ Networking Mistakes: Maximize your Networking Efforts by Avoiding Common Mistakes,* Tiffanie has been sharing referral marketing secrets with entrepreneurs for a decade.

Whether she is delivering keynote presentations, training and speaking here locally, or working with people in her Referrals for Life® community, Tiffanie loves helping entrepreneurs create the life they desire!

Her secret to success is LOVING what she does, and her goal is to leave it to others to decide whether she is working or playing...

Today, Tiffanie is going to help us save some time while making money and having fun!

Additionally, I often ask groups I am presenting for to use my "outro," either when I have finished my speech, before a break, or at the end of the event:

Be sure to stop by and see Tiffanie at _____ (point to where she is waiting with her books) on your break, to give her your "Tell Me More" sheet, purchase her book, or enroll in an upcoming program.

I know she will be happy to take photos with you and sign her books!

Your introduction helps the audience like you before you even step on the stage. You may want to hire a writer and/or editor to help you draft a powerful introduction.

#eTiffanie: Help the audience like you from the beginning with a well crafted and delivered intro.

How to Master Nervousness and Stage Fright

When polled about their fears, Americans consistently rate public speaking #1, ahead of even death! Now, I could understand if speaking in public ALWAYS led to an agonizing death. Fortunately, I have never heard of a single person who died from giving a presentation.

So why are people so afraid?

For some, being the center of attention and feeling the heat of the spotlight makes them uncomfortable. For others, it boils down to a fear of failure, of messing up and looking bad in front of a crowd. Those who lack experience simply fear the unknown. After all, it often takes several attempts at a new activity to feel comfortable with what we are doing.

Thankfully, there is a wealth of techniques for beating your nerves and overcoming your fear.

Evaluate Your Fear
The first thing you will want to do when dealing with the nervousness is evaluate what you are really afraid of.

Are you afraid of messing up during your presentation?
Do you think you might forget a section? Accidently reverse point 2 and point 3? Say 56 instead of 65? Here's the thing: the majority of the mistakes you might make during the presentation will be completely unnoticeable to the audience unless you tell on yourself. Even if the audience notices, most people really don't care about little errors – they happen to everyone. If you don't make a big deal about it, any mistake will probably not be the most memorable part of your speech.

Do you worry that people will not like you or your content?
We are typically our own worst critics – even I have delivered a presentation, then walked off stage criticizing myself for how poorly I did. Yet, afterwards, people came up to me to let me know how much they enjoyed the topic and ask to buy my book!
While we all want to be perfect with each word we say, with our tone, our movement, and our connection, the audience members themselves typically appreciate not having to be the ones on stage. This automatically endears them to you. Additionally, when the right person introduces you with a powerful bio, they help position the audience to like you before you even step on the stage. And shortly after you step in front of the room, you will be sharing your STORY, helping to connect them to you even more.

Are you just naturally nervous?
I know many Professional Members of NSA (National Speakers Association), and even some with decades of experience who get jittery before presentations. It is just

natural. However, they have learned that nervousness is simply energy to harness for their benefit.

Have you heard the analogy that feeling nervous is like having butterflies in your stomach? In *the Ignite your Business* Program, Asentiv® trainers share that the goal is to get the butterflies to fly in **formation**.

So, what can you do to soothe those butterflies?

Practice

Practicing your presentation is one of the best things I know that you can do to help with those nerves – so much so that we devoted Chapter 16 to it. As a reminder, practice builds confidence, and confidence can overpower nervousness.

Stress Busting Exercises

There are many techniques that people use to help get them in the mindset for presenting. You can:

- *Listen to music.* Some people prefer soft and soothing music to help create some "Zen," while other presenters prefer loud and upbeat music to "get up". Determine what kind of music would help you get in the right mindset and create your "pre-presentation" playlist.

- *Visualize your success.* Inside your mind, imagine what you will create with this presentation: the business and referrals that will flow to you, the standing ovation that you will receive at the end, the feeling that the audience just cannot get enough of what you have to say!

- *Utilize positive affirmations.* Send yourself positive thoughts of success.
  I have affirmations that I use before I get on stage each time, and if possible, I will say them out loud, though I often simply run through them in my head.
  NOTE: These affirmations MUST be positive! If you use negatives, for example: "I will not mess up", all your mind processes is "mess up." Choose hopeful words and avoid negatives!

- *Use Power Poses.* There is a great TEDTalk by Amy Cutty that explores using power poses (my favorite being Wonder Woman). Watch it online at <u>youtu.be/Ks- Mh1QhMc</u>.

- *Utilize Breathing Exercises.* There are various breathing techniques you can try to help you either calm down or get hyped to go on stage. Find the routine that best helps you balance yourself.

- *Meditate.* This may depend on where you are speaking. If there is a quiet space where you can prepare, it could be an option to help you gain your focus.

Try as many as you want and pick the technique(s) that work(s) best for you.

Engage the Audience

When you engage the audience, it helps them pay more attention to the program instead of locking their eyes on you. We devoted Chapter 12 and 13 to engaging your audience.

Make Eye Contact

There is power in connecting with your audience, and, when you make eye contact, you can see the people getting involved and interested in what you have to say. You will want to make contact with as many people, as often as possible – just find the ones who are the most engaged. Focus on those who are into what you have to say and present to them! Their attention is a kind of positive feedback that works as a great confidence booster and can help settle your nerves.

Have Cheerleaders

Okay, of course I am not talking about literal cheerleaders with skirts and pom-poms, though that would definitely make for an interesting presentation. I'm referring to people in the audience who you know will give you amazing visual feedback, like big smiles, thumbs ups, or even little signs with "YEAH!" or "GREAT!" written on them.

If possible, I recommend sprinkling these people strategically throughout the room, so that you will be able to move from one cheerleader to the next while scanning the audience in-between.

Not every person is meant to be a cheerleader. My husband is very even-tempered and rarely cracks big smiles. You want someone who will be over-the-top with their support and energy to let you know you are doing an amazing job!

Whether you choose to use a single technique from this chapter or several, know that some nervousness is good, natural, and nothing to worry about. I know many professional speakers (including myself) who still come down with "nerves" before big speeches. Nerves are energy. Use that energy to help *Knock the Socks off Your Audience*!

What Could Go Wrong?

In 2007, I was at a conference in Clearwater, Florida with a number of speakers. The opening portion of the day went over time, so the entire program was running behind. After a short break, we were headed to breakout sessions, where the audience got to choose a presentation from several, the event organizers asked the next group of speakers to shave their presentation by 10 minutes to help get the program back on schedule. In my breakout, the speaker started off by sharing that he had an hour presentation, and, just because the earlier section ran late, that didn't mean he should have to cut his speech short. Towards the end, as the meeting planner was trying to get him to finish, he again proclaimed that he had an hour to speak and would not leave until he was finished. People started coming in for the next section, but he shooed them out of the room.
Did anyone remember his content, his message, the actions he wanted us to take? No. He only left us with an impression of an egotistical, self-centered man.

As we discussed earlier, some people's fear of public speaking comes from obsessing over what could go wrong! In this chapter, I want to acknowledge that things can go wrong, and they sometimes do. However, the way you react to curveballs makes all the difference. You can either turn disaster into laughter or let it ruin the show! Let's look at how to make the best of a bad situation.

Time

This is at the top of the list for a reason. Delays happen all the time and speakers often find that their time gets cut.

It is important to know how much time you have and come in with a backup plan for the possibility of a shortened presentation. **NEVER** (yes, capitalized and bolded, because it means NEVER) cut your conclusion from your presentation! It is crucial to closing on a high note. Think about the parts you can reasonably cut while still getting your key points across, if necessary.

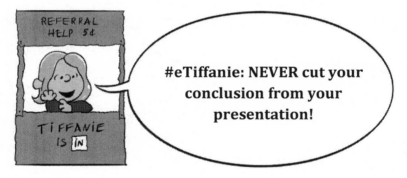

#eTiffanie: NEVER cut your conclusion from your presentation!

Technology Happens

There is almost no way to avoid relying on technology these days, particularly PowerPoint slideshows. Unfortunately, as you have surely experienced before, equipment can be iffy at times. With this in mind, I am often surprised that so many people are shocked when the projector doesn't work or the computer won't accept the USB drive or any other technical issues come up.

Recommendation? Bring a back up of your back ups! If tech is essential to your presentation, bring an extra projector, clicker, USB drive, or computer! Have the back up just in case. Always run through your presentation in advance, especially if you are putting files on someone else's computer. You never know if videos and animation will load correctly, and your slideshow may have fonts that other systems cannot read.

Remember what I said in Chapter 18 about being prepared? Consider this another reminder that you should always expect the unexpected!

Once in a while, you may have to do your presentation without technology, so be ready for that too! You will not be able to hold up copies of your slides for people to look at – who would be able to read a sheet of paper from the audience? Referencing charts or graphs won't work either. When you practice, be sure to dedicate some time to describing this type of content well, just in case nobody can see it.

Recently I was presenting for a women's group, and, though I had tested the PowerPoint, sound, clicker, and everything else before the audience arrived, my clicker stopped working. I had one of the Chamber of Commerce employees pop up to hit enter when I would point to her for the slide, which worked for a couple of slides. Then that stopped working too! So, I just shut the laptop and delivered the presentation without visuals. My fear was that continuing to fight the technical issues would have detracted from my speech, and I wanted the audience to stay focused on the message.

The Trip and Fall

Many people are afraid that they are going to trip and fall, or throw up, or pee their pants, so much so that over and over again in their head they are repeating "don't trip, don't trip, don't trip." The problem with the reoccurring mantra is that the brain does not process negatives very well. Because of this, all you are doing is telling your brain is, "Trip, trip, trip!" That's why this kind of fear often becomes a self-fulfilling prophecy.

A slight shuffle of the feet, or even a fall, is only as bad as you make it. I often think about toddlers beginning to walk. If they fall and their mom is around to react, they cry. If it seems like no big deal, no crying baby. The same can be said for public speakers. If you lose your footing and you react with extreme embarrassment, the audience will feel uncomfortable. If you act like it was no big deal, then the audience will move right on with you. If you treat it with humor, the audience will relax and find you more likable! While this situation is extremely unlikely, ease your worry by keeping this line in your back pocket: "I meant to do that!"

Forgetting what you wanted to say next

Life happens and sometimes you can go off-track during a presentation. If you tend to wander, consider keeping an outline or note cards with you to help you remember your cues. Some speakers rely on PowerPoint slides to keep them moving smoothly from one topic to the next. As I mentioned earlier, though, I typically use the slides to help make a point instead of reminding me of what is next.

Recently, I had an idea I wanted to share with an audience. I set them up for this great tip, and the tip flew from my brain. I thought for several seconds, but the thought still evaded me. I let them know we would come back to it, letting the suspense build, all the while hoping I would eventually remember what I wanted to say. Five minutes later, I finally did!

Hecklers

Sometimes you may come across an audience member who just can't stand being out of the spotlight for too long. Hopefully, this person will not try to steal the show, though I have seen it happen before. Interruptions can be as basic as questions or thoughts the audience member has, but they are still annoying and have the potential to derail your whole presentation.

How should you handle such a person?

Typically, I try to let people know up front whether they can ask questions or not during the presentation (depending on the type of presentation and the audience). For me, it truly depends on where I am speaking, what the topic is, and whether the agenda includes a question and comment section.
If people try to ask questions during the program simply let them know that you cannot answer questions here and now due to time constraints. Then, politely offer to be available afterwards or via email or to schedule an

appointment, so you can answer any questions the group may have.

If I have offered to answer questions during the presentation and end up dealing with someone who constantly interrupts with their own thoughts and comments, here is what I do:

When he or she continues to raise their hand, I will ask, "Do you have a question?" and, if the answer is no, I will tell them that we will come back for comments shortly, if possible.

You cannot help what the audience does sometimes, but you can always find ways to keep the momentum moving forward.

As with life, there are things that can go wrong during a presentation. The key is to keep a cool head and roll with the punches. The less energy that you expend on a mishap, the less your audience will care about it or even notice it.

After the Presentation

When the presentation is over, it does not mean that your job is done! If you are presenting because you want your audience to take action, then your speech is just the beginning.

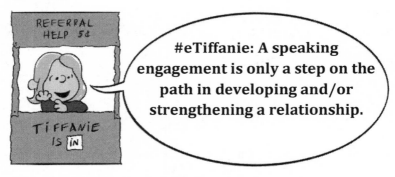

#eTiffanie: A speaking engagement is only a step on the path in developing and/or strengthening a relationship.

Immediately following any event where you speak, you will want to follow up!
If you promised the audience something, such as additional information or enrollment in a program, fulfill your promise quickly. The sooner you deliver, the more professional you will look.

It is also a good idea to follow up with the person who organized the event (and, if someone referred you, that person as well). Showing your gratitude and strengthening those relationships will help you land more speaking engagements in the future.

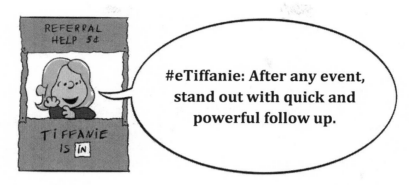

The Future

Is it possible to keep in touch with the group that booked you to keep track of your audience members? Do you have a system for staying in touch with those members, to hear how they implemented the information you gave in your speech?

Dramatic change rarely happens in a single session. However, one good encounter can be the catalyst for change, especially if your listeners connect with you. Hearing about these people's results a week, a month, or a year down the road can give you good feedback on whether your content is effective and you are getting the results you set out to get!

What impact are YOU creating?

The End...

Thank you for sticking through right to the end! We hope you have gained a few new tricks to help you reach your goals. Presenting can be a powerful way to deliver your message to a wider audience and grow your business.

Here are some key concepts I want to leave you with:

What is the intention of your presentation – and how will you get it to flow throughout your speech?

The goal is to magnetize your audience, turning a captive audience into a *captivated* one.

Share your STORY to help have the audience emotionally connect with you, beginning a powerful relationship.

Deliver with power, passion, and a call to action.

And be sure to follow up!

Remember, you can always look back at the **#eTiffanie**s as you move forward for a quick reference.

Now, go out there and ***KNOCK THE SOCKS OFF YOUR AUDIENCE***!

Any Questions?

Why might you contact me? For any reason you want! You can hire me as a consultant, schedule a coaching call to work on your STORY, book me to speak to your company or organization, request information on an upcoming program, or just ask additional questions.

If you want to learn more about me, visit my website: www.tiffaniekellog.com. You can also reach me at referrals@tiffaniekellog.com.

Tiffanie's Presentation Topics:

- *Knock the Socks off Your Audience*
  During this engaging presentation, I will share pieces of the book that you are holding in your hand!

- *4 1/2 Networking Mistakes*
  There are 4 ½ networking tips that experts tell you to perform EVERY DAY, and they are WRONG! Your nametag may be hurting instead of helping you and that elevator speech probably has people running the other way. Join Tiffanie Kellog as she explores the *4 ½ Networking Mistakes that Even*

the Experts Make and discover a few alternatives that will help you network more effectively.

- *Networking for Results*
  Networking is a MUST for so many entrepreneurs, yet many do it without focus. Why? Some people are simply uncomfortable when networking. Most others are discouraged when they never get the results they want.

  When done properly, networking can be a great way to meet new potential referral sources and clients. During this presentation, participants will explore the 19 Networking Nuggets and learn what to do before, during, and after a networking event, so they can begin networking with focus. We will also cover tips for dealing with nervousness for those who feel uncomfortable when networking.

- *5 Steps to Referral Success*
  During the *5 Steps to Referral Success* program, Tiffanie explores the simple steps necessary to create a steady flow of referrals for your business. Tiffanie will answer:

  > • Who could be passing you MORE referrals?
  > • What do you need to do to make it easier for people to pass you referrals?
  > • How can you develop stronger relationships with the people in your network, and how can this inspire them to pass you more business?

- What are the best ways to ask for referrals?

Participants will finish the program ready to go out and get additional referrals for their business!

- *How to Double or Triple your Referrals in the Next 60 to 90 Days*

- *Filling your Referral Pipeline*

- *10 Commandments of Networking*

- *Playing + Networking = RESULTS*

- *Your Target Market & Finding Your Starting Point*

- *Creating & Delivering an Effective Presentation*

- *Face to Face Networking + Online Networking = Results*

- *Branding Brilliance: Exploring How to Make YOU Your Own Brand*

Other Places You Can Find Me

You can follow and connect with me via social media:

www.facebook.com/TiffanieSpeaks
www.linkedin.com/in/tiffaniekellog
YouTube: Tiffanie Kellog

For over a decade, I have been associated with Asentiv®, formally known as the Referral Institute. This company offers several programs that help entrepreneurs create amazing businesses so they can live amazing lives.

117

To learn more about the company, as well as the programs we offer, you can visit Tampa.Asentiv.com.

In addition, I highly recommend these books if you are looking to further develop your skills as a presenter:

- *The Presentation Secrets of Steve Jobs: How to Be Insanely Great in Front of Any Audience* by Carmine Gallo

- *TEDTalks Storytelling: 23 Storytelling Techniques from the Best Ted Talks* by Akash Karia

- *PresentationZen: Simple Ideas on Presentation Design and Delivery* by Garr Reynolds

- *Start with Why: How Great Leaders Inspire Everyone to Take Action* by Simon Sinek

Of course, if you have not read it yet, my first book is a great read for people who like to network to grow their business, *4 ½ Networking Mistakes: Maximize your Networking Efforts by Avoiding Common Mistakes*. It is available on Amazon at:

http://bit.ly/4halfmistakes

There are 3 organizations I would also like to recommend:

- Toastmasters (www.toastmasters.org) – an amazing organization and a great tool for developing your talents in front of a roomful of people.

- NSA (National Speakers Association – www.nsaspeaker.org) – become a member here if you want to pursue a career as a public speaker.

- BNI (Business Network International - www.bni.com) – if you are an entrepreneur looking to develop your business, this organization pairs you with like-minded individuals who seek to grow by referral. BNI is the reason I originally started speaking and will always hold a warm space in my heart.

Bonus Material

As promised, here is the Bonus Material - I hope this is helpful!

Topics are:

- People sharing their STORIES
- Presentations for BNI Members
- The Platinum Rule®

Bonus Material: Additional Stories

My Twitter Twitters Version
In March of 2003, two things happened to help get me where I am today. 1st, I lost my job through corporate restructuring. 2nd, my mother who had spent the past 17 months battling breast cancer, was given a terminal diagnosis.

Luckily, I was able to spend the last 3 ½ months with my mom each and every day. That time, the memories, are precious to me... I became an entrepreneur to be able to live life to the fullest, which is what I do with the people I work with. My goal is to help people have an amazing business so they can live spectacular lives

My Cliffnotes Version
I grew up in the country, with no neighbors nearby, so I was very close to my family. We moved to Charlotte, NC when I was in high school, and I staying in the Queen City for college. I got into the real world, got the real job, and went to work. In March of 2003, though, two things happened that dramatically impacted my life. 1st – my job, through a Board restructuring, was eliminated, and I was offered a severance package. 2nd – my mother, who had been battling breast cancer for the past 17 months, was given a terminal diagnosis. They were stopping all treatments and said we might only have a couple of weeks left.

As to the first, being unemployed actually ended up being one of the best things that every happened to me. I was able to spend the last 3 ½ months with my mom, every single day. Some days it was just crawling in bed with her to watch her favorite judge shows, while on others, if she felt better, she would come out to the family area and spend time with us. Just a few days after her 47th birthday, she passed away in her sleep.

I was left wondering what I was going to do with my life. I had no job, and I had just lost my best friend. There was a friend of the family, Jackie, who would come over and visit during the week because she was an entrepreneur and made her own schedule. Everyone else could only come over at night or on the weekend, because they had 9-5 type jobs. I decided that I wanted the same freedom that Jackie had in my own life! I picked up my life in North Carolina and moved down to Florida to start my own business. I quickly learned, though, that, just because I had a business, it didn't mean I had any business coming through the door. After spending almost 2 years of weeks filled mostly with cold calling, I discovered networking and fell in love. In 2006, I took the Certified Networker Program, which dramatically change the way I was doing business, and I finally had more freedom in my schedule, a steady flow of income, and I was able to get my husband to quit his job and come work with me.

Because of the impact the program had on my life, I started training with the Certified Networker Program and other Asentiv programs, because I realized that I wanted to create for others what the program had created for me!

Now, I work with entrepreneurs to create the life they desire, if not today, then definitely as soon as possible.

We don't know what will happen in the future, so I help people live life to the fullest now.

Today, I work with entrepreneurs to help them have amazing businesses and spectacular lives.

Rick Saltarelli of Cruise Planners
(www.saltybreezecruiseplanners.com):

Growing up, I dealt with being in and out of the orphanage several times and was in my second foster home when I was 10 years old.

I remember when, even though I was showered with love, there wasn't time for family vacations because we were on a farm with chores to do. While I have many pleasant memories, there weren't a lot of memories based around great family vacation experiences. One of the reasons I enjoy my current work so much is the ability that I have to help busy families create lifelong lasting memories, regardless of their vacation budget.

Denice McClure of Florida Power Yoga
(www.floridapoweryoga.com)

Remember seeing huge Jungle Gyms with high wooden towers, long swinging bridges, and yellow spiral slides in almost every backyard in the 90's? I always thought it was weird that you never saw kids playing on them. Where were they? Why weren't the kids playing on them? If I had one, I would've been in the top tower as the Captain of the largest pirate ship in the sea! Not just any sea but a sea filled with 50 foot crocodiles. My friends would've been chanting "Walk the Plank, Walk the Plank!" as each of us hoped to be the one to dive into the sandbox below to fight the crocs. Yet these structures were unused. Not a kid in sight.

To me, they stood as a big, sad monument of the time when kids stopped learning how to play. Parents started putting themselves second so they could rush their children from dance lessons to music lessons to little league to cheer to movies with pizzas you could order while you watched. Playtime and family time got replaced with busy calendars. Busy, Rush, Can't: These were the new four letter words defining our culture.

Before I opened my doors, I wondered: "Have kids truly forgotten how to play? Have parents forgotten how much fun they had growing up with their friends?" These unused structures opened my eyes to a real need. We need, as a culture, to re-learn how to play again.

When I was growing up, my parents didn't make a lot of money. But I didn't know. I was having too much fun playing outside with my friends. We were building forts, forming clubs, climbing trees, playing hide & seek or dodge ball. My dad was an educator with a generous heart and a creative mind, and was great with his hands. For our birthdays, he built my sister and I the biggest sand box you could ever imagine. He put it together with 36 4x4 railroad ties he got from the junk yard for free. One by one he carried them on the roof of his car, and hauled the sand in from Walnut Beach. Back and forth he went, with load after load of sand. This wasn't a case of opening a 50 pound bag of sand up and dumping it in. He probably brought in a ton with at least ten trunk loads and one very angry mom.

Let me tell you about this sandbox, as it was no ordinary sandbox! It had three tiers so that trucks could leap from level to level or we could create sand water fountains. We didn't have pink, yellow or blue sand pails with cute green racks and shovels. We had 5 gallon buckets he found in a dumpster behind the local lumber yard; these originally contained something black and gooey that he had to wash out for days. He would tell us that 5 gallon buckets build strong castles to provide solid foundations. We had PVC pipes that he split in half as our shovels. Boy, could they scoop huge amounts of sand at once. Every kid in our neighborhood was in that sandbox from the time we were released from breakfast until the street lights came on.

We were messy, filthy, stinky kids that loved to play. Before dinner, we got the order to jump into the tub. The bath water went from clear to muddy in seconds. Once we made it to the dinner table, we had lots to talk about with our parents, especially regarding the conversations we had with other kids. I remember having the best laughs and conversations in that sandbox. In fact, I think I learned about love and sharing in that sandbox. We most assuredly became experts on sex as one of the older girls informed us that the barnacle had the largest penis for its tiny body weight. There were lots of poop conversations too – what seven year old isn't obsessed with poop? I felt like there were endless possibilities of things we could create together. We discovered that things need to have solid, strong foundations to last because the mean boy down the street would often come and kick over our castles. That happened a few times until we learned to combine girl power by challenging him to inhale deeply and eat a hot pepper from my dad's garden. Maybe that's why I like a hot environment now. We become powerful against any struggle when we breathe through the struggle. That boy ran home like a crying newborn wanting more food. I felt like the people in my sandbox were friends I would have for life, and most of them are today, besides maybe Pepper Boy. It was my sandbox. Yet, when we were together as friends, it was all of ours to play in. The messier we were together, the more fun we had.

What I realize today is that play is one of life's greatest gifts. It helps to keep our minds child-like, our bodies mobile, and our births our ability to make lifelong friends. It teaches that the purpose of generosity is for others to know God. We as a culture may have gotten sidetracked with busy lives, leaving unused structures behind our houses, yet we can always hit a RE-START Button when we find the option to play.

Today, my most vivid final memory of my dad was of him making a huge pot of hot cocoa for a group of high school kids as they were building a gazebo in the winter years. This was just before he passed away at the age of 85. He had nothing to put the hot coco in. Out of nowhere, he starts pouring it in Wal-Mart Bags. We laughed so hard together. When he brought it out for the kids, he cut a small hole in the bag and the chocolate poured in a simple fluid stream. And that, my friends, is generosity. We are filled to overflow with goodness. My dad raised every penny to build this beautiful gazebo in a park for the town to enjoy.

The gazebo was his sandbox. As his funeral procession passed the gazebo on that cold blizzard day in 2011, I thought about how similar my sandbox was to his gazebo. The lessons I learned in my sandbox from my dad's generosity are the very lessons I teach my friends about how to fall in love with getting messy. I teach how to have fun getting messy with your friends and soon-to-be new friends. And most importantly, I teach people how to slow down and prioritize themselves with play, as it keeps all aspects of our health in check. I teach them to sit on the swing, and learn to push themselves again! When I am teaching, I am back in my sandbox with all of my friends playing. Sometimes the moment is so strong that I imagine sitting with my dad, drinking a hot cup of cocoa as we watch my friends play together and laugh when we mention Pepper Boy's name, as he must have a funny story to tell his daughters now about how his bullying days were ended by a few small but mighty girls who knew how to play hard, get messy and swing like there was no tomorrow. And this is why I do what I do!

Mrs. Diane Emery DiMaggio, owner of Executive Reporting Service (www.executivereporting.com)

Let me tell you why I do what I do. Growing up in Tampa in 5th grade I had the best group of girlfriends. We did everything together. My best friend was the ring leader of our group, and I wanted to be just like her. She was bold, strong, had the cutest brothers, and a great family. All the boys liked her and all the girls wanted to be like her. One day at dinner, I received a phone call and I got up from the dinner table to answer the phone (this was before cell phones – we had an old fashioned dial phone with a cord). When I answered, Susie Smith (name changed to protect the innocent), my best friend, was screaming in the phone. I remember looking out the glass doors and across the lake to our elementary school, trying to figure out why she was so upset.

All of a sudden, I realized what she was saying. Someone had spray-painted in large black letters across the end of our 5th grade wing, "Susie Smith stuffs her bra."

I looked and could see the painting from across the lake – that's how big the letters were. I was shocked. Then it got even worse as I realized Susie was accusing me of being the one who did it. Then I was horrified.

A sinking, heavy feeling came across my chest once I realized that Susie thought I would do something that awful. Reasoning with her only made it worse as I tried to tell her I had no idea who would do such a thing or think such a thing. No matter what I said, she just would not believe me.

The next day at school none of the girls would talk to me. I remember turning cold and numb, and at that moment I decided I was never going to get close to girls again, nor would I trust them. I decided I didn't need anybody and could do things on my own.

Looking back, I can see how this experience shaped everything that came after, and how it was one of the elements that made court reporting such an attractive career. Court reporters capture spoken words and turn them into written words that become evidence to protect the innocent. My mission is to leave my clients knowing that I've got their back, that I will preserve and document every detail to protect them in the future and give them peace of mind. That's why I do what I do.

Mickey Griffith with Asentiv (sfbay.asentiv.com)

I suppose that if I'm going to share *why* I love what I do, I should first describe *what* it is that I do. I am a business coach with a background of more than twenty years in marketing communications. As an Asentiv franchise owner, and an expert in relationship marketing, I get to help people build their businesses in a way that brings out their passion and helps them live an abundant life. I do that by presenting classroom programs, public speaking, and one-to-one coaching.

The reason *why* I do what I do is really my mother's fault.

For my entire life, my mother called me her sunshine. She sang "You Are My Sunshine" to me more times than I could count and even wrote it on my lunch bags. It's no mystery why I am the way I am. My mother and my grandmother are both loud laughers and big huggers. They, along with my aunt, were very doting and loving people. In my childhood it was very easy to find praise and joy with them.

In contrast, my stepfather was a devout alcoholic. While he was very, very rarely physically abusive, he was consistently verbally abusive. For every time my mother praised something I had done or had a kind word about a personal quality of mine, he was right there to tell me how stupid I was and that I would never amount to anything. I spent the entirety of my childhood with my mother trying to undo all of the negative input I got from him.

One place that I did very well was school. Not by way of bragging, but it came easy to me. This is probably because my mother was always reading to me. We did lots of crossword puzzles, word searches, brain games, IQ tests, etc., and I was reading before I ever went to school. My mother became a teacher in my high school years, working with Kindergarten and 1st grade students, and I went to the very small private school that she worked at.

The teachers would often ask me to work with another student if they were having a hard time and I was happy to help. I remember one time working with a quiet, nervous little kindergartner named Debbie Litton. She was a doe-eyed, sandy-haired, tiny little thing that was very shy and having a hard time with basic beginning math. I was helping her and ran into a lot of difficulty getting her to understand the concept of 2+3, 4-1, etc. In frustration, I grabbed a handful of popsicle sticks and put them on the desk. I took her little hand in mine and pointed her finger at each stick while we walked through it. We were right in the middle of counting through another example when she snapped her head around and looked me at me with a big grin and wide eyes. Seeing the light come on, knowing that she had grasped the material and that I had helped her do it was immensely satisfying. I couldn't wait to tell my mother and the other teachers.

The only way to describe how it felt to see Debbie's eyes light up is "goosebumps." It still gives me goosebumps today. Knowing that I was the person that helped open the door to understanding, and seeing it brighten up her face – that was a feeling that I wanted to experience every day of my life. Later, the school faculty would tell me that Debbie started to open up more after that. It still makes me smile to think about her running across the parking lot in the mornings to give me a hug and say hello.

After high school, I went into the US Navy for nearly six years. I had the privilege of serving on the USS Missouri BB63. During my tour on the Missouri I was given the responsibility of setting up a computer center and teaching others how to use them. It was a great challenge learning how to present material and manage relationships with people of every rank. The way you communicate with high ranking officers may be quite different than your basic deck hand. Then, while on the Missouri, I was deployed to the first Persian Gulf conflict in 1990. My mother made a recording of her singing "You

Are My Sunshine" and sent to me. She was funny that way and we made fun of her for it as children will do, but it really makes me smile now.

My mother and I continued our educational relationship after the internet became available. We did personality tests online, played Scrabble, and exchanged brain teasers. And somehow, throughout my career, I always seemed to find myself in a position of instructing others.

On June 5, 2011, my mother passed away after a long battle with lung cancer. She was living in southern Utah with my stepfather, and my sister was there every step of the way to support her. As I was in California, I didn't get much opportunity to go see her. We talked by phone and video as often as we could.

In January of 2011, Mom was still in the struggling with chemo when she developed a case of diverticulitis and something inside of her burst. I'm sure there were more details than that, but I didn't want to hear them. They told me that half of those that are normal, healthy people do not survive the surgery and that I should come see her. When I got the hospital, I hadn't not even gotten to my mother's room before my sister-in-law managed to get under my skin. By the time I got to see my mother, I was complaining about my sister-in-law instead of worrying about Mom. She told me to be patient; to have grace. She explained that I did not know my sister-in-law's entire life story and that I should be kind to her. This was just one of many examples of how my mother tried to live. Here she was, in post surgery, with tubes running in and out of her body, with me complaining like a little kid, and she had the presence of mind to continue coaching me on managing relationships. Even the ones I didn't want to manage.

I flew back to Utah again for Mom's funeral in June. I couldn't get up to speak, though I wanted to. I can remember that it was everything she would have wanted in a service. She had a big group of people there to say goodbye.

When I returned to my life, I understandably found that things were not the same. The biggest problem I had was work. My family and friends were all amazing and supportive, but I could not get my head wrapped around my daily duties. I had a successful, profitable marketing communications firm. I had doubled my business every year for three years and we were doing a lot of good work. That all changed when I came back. I found myself staring at my computer for weeks. It seemed impossible to work on another website, or a brochure, or a business card.

I kept thinking back to may mother's funeral and something finally dawned on me. Many of the people that I remember getting up to say goodbye to my mother were very young people, in their early twenties or late teens. They had all come to say goodbye to somebody who had impacted their lives for years. They had all been students of hers in Kindergarten and 1st grade.

All of my life, I thought I was just Sunshine. I had been born that way. Just popped out and here I was. What I realized is that shining was not something I just had, it was a gift my mother gave me. And not just me. She had given it to so many others as well. These young people were all shining, and I think in no small part that was because of her.

I realized then that if I were going to honor my mother's memory, I needed to live my life helping others shine in whatever way I could. I also needed to find a way to do that in business. I had some opportunities with my clients to do that through marketing, but it wasn't the websites or printed materials that I really was passionate about. I was energized by hearing their stories, seeing their passion, and finding a way to help them bring that to other people.

Today, as an Asentiv franchise owner, I have the opportunity to help people shine in their own unique way every day. And when they do, they attract the kind of clients, referral sources, employees, and partners that bring them an amazing business and a spectacular life. Every time I see a client improve their businesses, and through it, their lives, I see them light up and smile about it. Every time, I think about how Debbie's eyes popped open and I get goosebumps. Every time, I think about how proud my mother would be to know that I am doing my best to pass on what she gave to me. And <u>that</u> is why I love what I do.

Christopher Clarke, owner of Therapeutic Elements Center for Massage Therapy (www.palmharbormassagetherapy.com)

My earliest memories of my parents are in Lakeland, FL where they owned a cute little craftsman style house on an old brick road, with a mother in-law apartment above a two car garage. In one half of the two-car garage, my mother, Carolyn, ran an upholstery business. She and my father, Tom, would drive around finding old furniture that people had discarded out on the curb and bring it back to her upholstery shop to fix up and sell to pay bills.

She would rip an entire couch all the way down to the wooden frame. Then she would carefully replace the broken springs and mechanisms. After some colorful language and a few projectile springs bouncing off the walls of the garage, my mother would recover the cushions with new fabric and finish her work by sewing brand new buttons on the seat cushions. No matter how it looked coming in, she could take any old, worn-out piece of furniture and make it look and feel brand new again. And after she completed each endeavor, she would gather the family to unveil her latest creation. The sense of pride was palpable as she'd exclaim, "Look what I did!"

As the caretakers of our own bodies, we own the most sophisticated and complex piece of machinery on the planet. However, we don't get a user manual and we definitely don't get a warranty. As your warranty repair professionals, we feel an immense sense of pride by making you look and feel brand new again. When you walk into Therapeutic Elements you may feel like an old worn out piece of furniture, but when you leave our office in a massage-drunken daze, we all silently think to ourselves, "Look what I did..."

Dr. Marnita E. Sandifer, owner of Spa Café (www.spacafe.biz)

Growing up, I felt like no one ever saw me. I always wanted to be picked first for study group, sports or clubs, but I was usually last. I would raise my hand to answer a question in class, and the teacher would look right past me to call on a student who didn't even have his hand up.

I remember in my Home Economics class, sewing was something that I really enjoyed and felt that I was really good at it. The project that I chose was a fringed skirt with trimming. I always picked patterns that would challenge my skill and level of creativity. When I completed the project, I really felt proud. I had dealt with some challenges that had to do with the fine details and considered it to be one of my best pieces. To my surprise, the grade I received was a D. I was incredibly disappointed, to say the least.

As a result, I wondered what the point was of trying. Nobody saw me.

Nobody, other than my parents, thought I would do anything with myself.

What I do today is to give my clients permission to stand out with confidence and inspiration. I want to help them discover the vision of what they can be. Life is a lot more fun, meaningful, and powerful when we are seen.

Bonus Material: BNI Members

When I first joined BNI in 2005, I was terrified to speak in front of a group for 30 seconds, let alone 10 minutes or more. Through BNI, I tackled my fear of presentations and now enjoy working as a professional speaker.

In this chapter, I will share BNI specific Do's and Don'ts. I have seen thousands of BNI Featured Presentations, many of them outstanding. I have also seen speakers make almost every mistake that can be made in a BNI presentation.

Throughout this book we have been exploring tips for speaking in general. This chapter specifically addresses the needs of BNI members preparing for a Featured Presentation.

#eTiffanie: In BNI, you have the opportunity to train your network to effectively refer you via your Featured Presentations, Weekly Presentations, and One to Ones.

Depending on the size of your chapter, you may only have the opportunity to speak 1-4 times a year. As such, you have plenty of time to plan in advance. Remember, you plan so you can deliver your presentation with power and passion, compelling the audience to like you. With your Featured Presentation, I always recommend that you start with some version of your *STORY*, whether it is 30 seconds or 3 minutes.

What else should be in your Featured Presentation? For BNI, two additional pieces are an absolute MUST for your Featured Presentation: success stories and a strong call to action.

Too often, members spend the majority of their time talking about their personal history, WHAT they do, or the products and services they offer. Instead, focus on the *benefits* to your clients. If you can successfully wrap the benefits into a story that shares how you have helped your clients, people will be much more likely to remember what you said and share it with others!

#eTiffanie: **The goal of a successful referral marketing plan is to inspire others to speak positively on your behalf, creating BUZZ!**

With your Call to Action, please offer us a few ideas that help us help you grow your business. These may include: asking for introductions to prospects and referral sources, requesting testimonials and speaking engagements, and soliciting invitations to networking meetings and events.

Tying all the pieces together is one of my favorite presentations for BNI, and it is called the 3, 3, 3. During this presentation, you spend 1/3 of your time sharing your STORY, 1/3 of the presentation sharing a couple of success stories, and wrapping up the presentation with the final 1/3, your Call to Action.

This is my personal favorite for generating referrals, though there are numerous additional formats that can accomplish the same thing for you.

Here are my Do's and Don'ts for Featured Presentations:

Do

- The #1 thing to do in all your presentations is to share the STORY of why you do what you do! Yes, I know I mentioned it before, it is important enough to include a second time.

- SUCCESS STORIES!!! These can be powerful and convincing. Be sure to include plenty of details – they help paint a picture and bring your words to life.

- Always have a Door Prize. This is actually policy #8: *"Speakers must bring a door prize. Only members bringing a visitor or a referral are eligible for the door prize."* Give serious consideration to this component, as it speaks volumes about your intention.

- Have a strong call to action: be specific on how we can help you!

- Teach us **how** to refer you and **whom** you want to be referred to!

- Use handouts *only* if you are going to address their content or have people write in them during your presentation.

- Have a powerful introduction and know that any member of your chapter can introduce you. Pick someone that knows you well and can speak positively about you.

Don't:

- Run over your time. In BNI, the bell doesn't tell you to stop talking, it tells the audience to stop listening! Manage your time to build your credibility.

- Tell people you did not prepare. This is a great way to kill your trustworthiness. Think about it. You are basically saying, "I knew 6 weeks in advance that I was speaking, but I couldn't find a single minute to get ready." The audience may be concerned about how you will respond if or when they have a chance to pass you a referral.

- Spend all your time talking about personal information (like family and pets).

- Ask for questions. I have seen in-presentation audience questions derail many presentations. Sometimes you get surprise questions that they are not ready to answer. Other times, there is no one correct answer (meaning "it depends"), which leads to long, complicated explanations or confusion. If your topic is highly specialized, detailed discussions can lose audience members who don't speak your jargon.

In 2005, my first year in BNI, I remember watching a financial advisor deliver a rather technical presentation that was a bit dry and hard to follow. Towards the end, he opened the floor and an insurance agent asked a question. I could not even follow what he was asking, much less make sense of the response. Instead, because I was no longer paying attention, I watched the audience. What I witnessed was the glazed-over expressions of so many others that the presenter had lost.

- Pass out your collateral material.
  An advertising sales person did her presentation in the spring. At the start, she passed out a copy of the newspaper she sold advertising for. Result? For the rest of the presentation, the audience read the paper instead of listening to her.

- Sell to the members. If there are members in the chapter who are interested in becoming clients of yours, they will ask! Your goal is to sell THROUGH the members, not TO them.

- Teach us HOW you do what you do.
  Another poor BNI presentation I saw involved a mortgage broker who spent her Feature Presentation explaining how FICA scores were derived. Snoozefest.

Remember the DOs and DON'Ts for BNI presentations, and deliver with power and passion to inspire the members to refer you! For additional information on BNI in your area, visit www.BNI.com.

Bonus Material: Behavioral Styles
from 4 ½ Networking Mistakes

Some of the best tips for networking begin with understanding who you are and what your strengths are. When we realize what it is that we bring to each conversation, we can see how to adapt in that conversation to make it an incredible experience for all involved. At the Referral Institute®, we have identified four major behavioral styles (based on the DiSC® profile). Let's share them with you so you can understand who you truly are.

Go-Getters

Definition: A hustling, enterprising type of person. The Go-Getter would be the equivalent of the "D" in the DiSC® language.

Go-Getters tend to be very results-oriented, driven, fast-paced and in many cases impatient. They have a "get it done now" attitude. They attend networking events to gain new business and look to meet the most successful people at the event. They tend to be very challenge-oriented and speak with very few words because they can be more productive with fewer words. They are not afraid to bend the rules. They figure it is easier to beg forgiveness than to ask permission. They are so focused that they can even appear aloof or unapproachable.

While networking, Go-Getters will tend to manage the conversation. They seek to understand what might be "attractive" about continuing the conversation with you and as long as you are competent, succinct, and intriguing, they are in!

If you would like a conversation that makes you attractive to them, include some of these questions emphasizing how you can help them, and then **do it**!

- What are the best clients for you?

- Which professions refer you most often?

- What are three business goals I might be able to help you with?

As you can see, these are very specific and geared to the Go-Getter's benefit. Here is the thing, if you give them some type of result quickly, they will find you "attractive." Receiving results are very important to them. The key here is that once you have shown Go-Getter results, they are much more committed to doing something for you. See, they also have a strong desire to win; so, in the language of giving referrals, they will want to give more to you whenever possible.

Promoters

Definition: An active supporter, someone who urges the adoption of, or attempts to sell or popularize someone or something. The Promoter would be the equivalent of the "I" in the DISC® language.

Promoters tend to be very positive, friendly, and "happy go lucky" people. They love to be on the go and are okay with having lots of irons in the fire. They avoid confrontation and seek fun in everything they do.

Promoters can be easily distracted and would rather go to lunch with clients or referral sources than work on a deadline in the office. They tend to utilize their enthusiasm and excitement to influence others. They are risk-takers who are not inclined to do their homework or check out information, and base many of their decisions on intuition.

While networking, Promoters like to hang out, meet new people, talk to their friends and make sure they are "seen" at the event. They enjoy connecting people and even being the life of the party.

Ask these types of questions to be seen as someone they will enjoy talking to and, ultimately, building a deeper relationship with.

- What do you love about what you do?
- What do you do for fun when you aren't working?
- Do you have favorite clients... if so, what do they look like?
- Who would you love to meet while you are here networking?

These types of questions will keep the conversation upbeat, fun, and enjoyable for them, which in turn will have them wanting to spend more time with you.

Nurturers

Definition: Someone who gives tender care and protection to a person or thing, especially to help it grow or develop. The Nurturer would be the equivalent to the "S" in the DiSC® language.

Nurturers tend to be very patient, kind, caring, and helpful people. They are great listeners and tend to enjoy things at a slower pace than the Go-Getters and Promoters. They do not liked to be pushed or rushed, and appreciate quality time with people. They attend networking functions to connect with people they already know, meet a few down-to-earth people and focus on deepening their relationships.

Nurturers have relaxed dispositions, which make them approachable and warm. They develop strong networks of people who are willing to be mutually supportive and reliable. They are excellent team players due to their supportive attitude.

You can ask these types of questions to begin developing a strong relationship with them.

- How long have you lived in the area?
- Where is your family located?
- What got you started in your business?
- Tell me what you enjoy most about your business?
- What type of clients do you enjoy working with the most?
- What is the long-term benefit of clients working with you?

As you can see, these types of questions evoke even more conversation, allowing you to go deeper into who they are and what they really enjoy. Do spend enough time with them so they feel like they got to know you. They are more concerned about who you are than what it is you do.

Examiners

Definition: A person who inspects or analyzes a person, place or thing in detail, while testing their knowledge or skill by asking questions. The Examiner would be the equivalent of the "C" in the DiSC® language.

Examiners tend to be very thorough, efficient, task-driven people. They seek information and knowledge, and love to check things off their "to do" list. Because Examiners need a lot of information, they tend to make decisions more slowly than the Go-Getters and Promoters. They have a propensity toward perfectionism.

While networking, Examiners tend to be very good conversationalists as they know a lot about a lot of topics. They attend networking functions only to market their business and, once they achieve their goal for the evening, they usually leave as quickly as they can. Whenever possible they like to have a job to do at the function, helping with registration, timekeeping, etc. This allows them to have something to do while they network and is much more comfortable for them.

You can ask them these types of questions to learn more about them:

- What do you do?

- How long have you been doing it?

- What is your specialty?

- Which types of clients do you prefer to work with?

- Are there strategic professions that often refer you?

Hopefully, by now you can see a bit of a trend in the questions, and yet just changing a few things make the questions more pertinent to each of the styles. Knowing this while networking can prove to be incredibly valuable to you in order to ensure you make the best impression you can!

Try to decide which behavioral style you would say is your highest style. Yes, you are a blend of all four styles, but if you had to declare one, which would it be? Okay, now that you know that, please utilize the strengths that we mention for your style even more! Using your strengths first will make networking very enjoyable and valuable to you and your business. In order to challenge yourself, ask some of those questions that appeal to the other styles more often. As you do, you will get more comfortable with them, attain better results while networking, make a better first impression, and definitely deepen and strengthen relationships more quickly!

It's that easy. To be a better networker, know yourself and the strengths you bring to the table in every conversation, and know other people's behavioral style, and watch as a better experience unfolds for all involved!

For more information on this material, please read the Amazon.com best-seller "Room Full of Referrals...and How to Network For Them" by Dr. Tony Alessandra, Dr. Ivan Misner, and Dawn Lyons.

Platinum Assessment® is registered to Dr. Tony Alessandra, an American best-selling author, entrepreneur and motivational speaker, an expertise in behavioral styles.

#eTiffanies

#eTiffanies

#eTiffanies

#eTiffanies

#eTiffanies

#eTiffanies

#eTiffanies

#eTiffanies

#eTiffanies